Few people understand grief the way Harold Ivan Smith understands it, and fewer still have the ability to write about it with such clarity and insight. To suffer loss while others are celebrating is a disorienting experience. This book is a healing gift to those whose pain seems out of place and intrusive. It is a welcome resource.

—Dr. Jesse C. Middendorf

Harold shares perceptive insights in how to deal with every part of the "Holiday" experience when viewed through the lens of grief. His words written with such empathy and realistic understanding eased my own memories of grief. Thank you, Harold, for caring enough to help us shape and create new pathways of meaningful celebration.

—Carolyn Lunn

The holidays and special days are special challenges, and if we let them be, invitations as we wander through the worlds of life and loss. Smith uses the perceptions of a skilled caregiver and author wrapped up in the integrity of his own genuineness from his loss experiences to bring us a good friend and a safe place in *A Decembered Grief.*

—Rev. Dr. Richard B. Gilbert,
executive director, The World Pastoral Care, author and speaker

This book will be an essential handbook for those who must endure holidays with fresh grief. Harold so poignantly provides a wealth of insights to flatten the pain we anticipate at the holidays.

—Barbara Johnson

Harold Ivan Smith is one of the Lord's true mystics. He takes us place we've never been and blesses us as we've never been blessed. This book is an absolute must.

—Dr. Charlie Shedd

*In Loving Memory of:*

_____

*Given by:*

_____

# A DECEMBERED Grief

Living with Loss
While Others Are
Celebrating

HAROLD IVAN SMITH

BEACON HILL PRESS
OF KANSAS CITY

ISBN 978-0-8341-2726-5

Printed in the
United States of America

Cover Design: Doug Bennett
Interior Design: Sharon Page

**Library of Congress Cataloging-in-Publication Data**

Smith, Harold Ivan, 1947-
  A Decembered grief : living with loss while others are celebrating / Harold Ivan Smith.
—Rev.
    p. cm.
  Includes bibliographical references (p.    ).
  ISBN 978-0-8341-2726-5 (hardcover)
  1. Bereavement—Religious aspects—Christianity. 2. Grief—Religious aspects—Christianity. 3. Christmas—Psychological aspects. I. Title.
  BV4905.3.S625 2011
  248.8'66—dc23
                                                        2011024825

10 9 8 7 6 5 4 3 2 1

# DEDICATION

My grief for my mother is only beginning . . .
how she loved the holidays,
how she loved to cook and to shop
and to wrap and to bake,
and most of all to surprise,
but who always said, always said,
"Honey, you shouldn't have . . ."
I lovingly dedicate this book to my mother,
Mary Catherine Eckert Smith
April 2, 1916—February 21, 1999

The phrase "Decembered grief" has taken on
a whole new meaning with her immigration
to the real country, where it is
Christmas every day!

# CONTENTS

# FOREWORD

*A*s you are no doubt painfully aware, holidays are often difficult for anyone who has experienced the death of someone loved. Rather than being times of family togetherness, sharing, and thanksgiving, holidays can bring feelings of sadness, loss, and emptiness. Since love does not end with death, holidays may result in a renewed sense of personal grief—a feeling of loss unlike that experienced in the routine of daily living. Society encourages you to join in the holiday spirit, but all around you the sounds, sights, and smells trigger memories of the person who died.

No book can take away the hurt you are feeling. I am confident, however, that the excellent suggestions in this compassionate text will help you better cope with your grief during this joyful, yet painful, time of the year.

The thousands of mourners I've had the privilege of meeting during my years as a grief counselor and educator have taught me that it helps to

- Talk about your grief.
- Be tolerant of your physical and psychological limits.
- Eliminate unnecessary stress.
- Be with supportive, comforting people.
- Talk about the person who has died.
- Do what is right for you.
- Plan ahead for family gatherings.
- Embrace your treasure of memories.
- Renew your resources for living.
- Express your faith.

Keep each holiday as a reminder of all the things you shared with the person who has died. And remember: grief is both a painful necessity and a privilege, for it comes as a result of having loved.

—Alan D. Wolfelt, Ph.D.
Director, Center for Loss and Life Transition
Author, *The Journey Through Grief: Reflections on Healing*

*If life experiences are not used—they are wasted.*
—Charlotte Czillinger
Following the murder of her teenage daughter
in "A Grief like No Other," 50

\* \* \*

*When one loses a significant other, even though*
*there may have been advanced warning of the death,*
*there's always a certain sense of unreality—*
*a sense that it did not really happen.*
*Therefore, the first grief task is to come*
*to a more complete awareness that*
*the loss actually has occurred—*
*the person is dead and will not return.*
*Survivors must accept this reality so they*
*can deal with the emotional impact of the loss.*
—J. William Worden
*Grief Counseling,* 42

\* \* \*

*Our lives have changed, but without our permission.*
—Elizabeth Harper Neeld
Seven Choices: Taking the Steps to New Life After Losing Someone You Love, by
Elizabeth Harper Neeld, 26. Copyright © 1990 by Neeld & Neeld, Inc. Reprinted
by permission of Clarkson N. Potter, a division of Crown Permissions, Inc.

\* \* \*

*God, I'm not asking for miracles throughout this season.*
*I'm asking to recognize Your movements in my life.*
*I'm asking to catch Your whispers. I'm asking*
*to sense Your presence in what I think are my*
*darkest moments, when I think I can't go on.*
*God, I'm asking for moments when I can see Your grace*
*as clearly as footprints in a fresh-fallen snow or wet sand*
*along a beach. God, I'm asking that You be with*
*my family and friends and somehow see us through.*

# INTRODUCTION

*O*nce upon a time a great king owned a beautiful diamond.

But there was a problem. The diamond had a flaw—a scratch in the middle. It could never be given, worn, or admired.

So the king, who was used to having his subjects make him happy, sent word throughout his vast kingdom that great riches, position, and prestige would come to any individual who could take away the flaw. Well, they came, the best of jewelers and artists, even magicians—not just from that kingdom, but from across the mountains and the seas. But alas—no one could remove the scratch. The king despaired.

Then one day a young man arrived, somewhat optimistic about his chances for doing what no one else had been able to do. Oh, he heard the doubters and the scoffers. But he asked for a quiet place to work where he would not be disturbed.

Every day the king asked, "Well?"

And the determined young man would answer, "Not yet."

Days passed. Weeks passed. Then one afternoon the young man handed the diamond to the king. Slowly a smile spread across the king's face, and then a great "Yes!" ricocheted through the palace. The queen, the courtesans, and the knights crowded in for a closer look.

The scratch was still there! But the young man had carved a rose around it, using the scratch for a stem.

—Adapted from Anne Brener
*Mourning and Mitzvah,* 231-32

You have had a deep scratch—no, a gash—inflicted on you. While you weep, while you wrestle with the realities of life without the one or ones you love, the world goes right on with the joys, the exuberance, the excitement, the frantic panic of the season. "Joy to the world" and "Ho! Ho! Ho!" Only your "Ho! Ho! Ho!" from previous years has turned into "Oh! Oh! Oh!" You've learned that it's possible as a griever to scream, "Christmas? Bah! Humbug!" in your soul; without a person sitting across from you at dinner or the person at the next workstation hearing a sound. You're wondering—really wondering—"Just how am I supposed to celebrate Christmas this year?" You may want to fast-forward to January 5 or yank the covers over your head, and snarl, "Wake me up when it's over." You, too, may identify with words in Henry Wadsworth Longfellow's carol:

> *And in despair I bowed my head.*
> *"There is no peace on earth," I said,*
> *"For hate is strong, and mocks the song*
> *Of peace on earth, goodwill to men."*

Longfellow penned those words during the long anguish called the Civil War. But he wrote a fourth (and fifth) verse. Otherwise, the song would not have become a seasonal favorite.

> *Then pealed the bells more loud and deep:*
> *"God is not dead, nor doth He sleep;*
> *The wrong shall fail, the right prevail,*
> *With peace on earth, goodwill to men."*

I write this book as a griever. I, too, have experienced seasonal loss. My grandfather died on Christmas Eve. I once worked as an apprentice embalmer in a funeral home on Christmas Eve and Christmas Day. I have led "grief gatherings" during the holidays at Saint Luke's Hospital in Kansas City. I have buried my father. I have buried friends. While writing this book, I buried my mother.

It is hard to do thorough grief work when there are so many distractions. Friends and family seem to invent ways to use the holiday buzz to detract you from your grief.

This book is an invitation—an invitation to Christmas and its companion holidays of the season, which compose a grueling triathlon that begins on Thanksgiving and continues unabated until the last of the bowl games on New Year's Day. The "Merry Christmas!" and "Happy New Year!" greetings will cause you to wince this year. No doubt, in previous years you relished the season, ready to instantly respond, "And merry Christmas to you too." But not this year.

I hope these quotes, prayers, scriptures, and reflections, plus the experiences of those who have journeyed beyond the shadow and directly into and through "the valley of death," will offer you some insight into the map of a grief-soaked season.

I cling to a carol phrase by Isaac Watts:

*He comes to make His blessings flow*
*Far as the curse is found.*

Yes, even *this* grief-filled season, He will come to you and will "make His blessings flow" through moments, through songs, through scents, through kind acts of caring people, through memories, through hopes.

I hope you will not snarl, lips clenched, "I will get through it somehow!" I hope you will turn it into a prayer: *Somehow, kind Jesus, lead me through this season.* I hope that in some distant day, you, too, will tell how you have overcome, that you will come alongside a fresh griever and say, "The holidays. Oh, yes—I've been there and survived!"

I would remind you that a widow is part of this Christmas story. How often we give only lip service to her involvement in the drama of Christmas! Try to find her in a carol or seasonal song. Anna was deliberately as much a part of the story as the wise men, the shepherds, the innkeeper, even the angels (Luke 2:36-38). I would remind you that the same Simeon who likely said, "Oh, what a cute baby!" when the parents presented Jesus in the Temple also said, "A sword will pierce your own soul too" (v. 35). I remind you that we cannot divorce Good Friday from Christmas. The Christmas story makes sense only when paired with the Easter story.

This is not any baby whose birth we celebrate. This is the Boy-child who would defeat our entrenched enemy, Death. This Infant would grow up to be described as Isaiah stated: "a man of sorrows, and acquainted with grief" (53:3, KJV), as Handel's text for a bass soloist reminds us in his well-known classic *Messiah*.

After experiencing grief, loss, and death (my own and the grief of those with whom I work as a grief counselor), I have come to believe in a Christmas that cannot be limited to 24 hours on the 25th of December. I have come to believe in a future Christmas when all of God's children will be home. I have come to believe that in our first moments in heaven we will realize how much He gave up to spend those years among us, to invite us to spend forever with Him. I believe that His coming locked this world into a loving embrace and that *this* December season He would be as close to us as a griever would allow.

# ALTER—RATHER THAN ABANDON—TRADITIONS

*Tears are a natural seasoning of the season.*

✳✳✳

*Life is the garment we continually alter,*
*but which never seems to fit.*
—David McCord
in *Familiar Quotations*, 839

✳✳✳

*Let the beloved of the LORD rest secure in him,*
*for he shields him all day long.*
—Deut. 33:12

✳✳✳

*If we can make a place where memories can be found,*
*again and again; where stories are told and retold; where*
*the special moments of our lives are visited again and*
*again; brought out of the closets and dusted off on the*
*shelves and walls and end tables; then we can make*
*a place where the Lord can remind us of the ways*
*His grace has found us.*
—Peggy Benson
Listening for a God Who Whispers: A Woman's Discovery of Quiet Understanding,
91. Copyright 1991 by Peggy Benson. Reprinted 1994
by Vaughan Printing and Solitude and Celebration Press.
Used by permission.

# "*We always . . .*"

Traditions are a great part of the glory of the three holidays: Thanksgiving, Christmas, and New Year's Day. When I was married, we had a tradition of making chili for friends on Thanksgiving eve. That first year alone, as I mulled over plans for a single Thanksgiving and wrestled with the "What to do?" question, I decided the tradition would continue—only in an altered format. So I made my first pot of chili ("Thank you, McCormick's!"), recruited five brave friends, and celebrated my first Thanksgiving without a spouse.

You may have a signature tradition in your family, something that your loved one dearly loved or perhaps even started. Should you go through with it?

While there are many people who are not deeply afraid of death, there are multitudes who are afraid of being forgotten. One way we actively remember is by including them through memories in our holidays, through keeping the tradition.

Perhaps you've always had a big home-cooked family dinner on Christmas Eve. This year the family could still gather, but maybe go to a restaurant. Or do a light meal, eaten on laps in the den or living room rather than at that memory-soaked dining room table. Or do an "everybody bring something."

The essence of the tradition—the family together on Christmas Eve—will be honored, but the setting altered. *This year.* Next year you can redecide.

One word of warning: Let people know of the change so they have time to get used to the idea of this specific alteration. Otherwise the "but we *always*" will overshadow the gathering.

\* \* \*

# ANTICIPATE THE HOLIDAYS

*Be guided by the reality that there is no
right or wrong way to celebrate the holidays
after a loved one has died.*

\* \* \*

*No matter what your religion may be, Christmas is all
around you, coming at you from all directions.*
—Helen Fitzgerald
*The Mourning Handbook,* 107

\* \* \*

*Christmas is not an easy time to do the work
of remembering, crying, feeling sad. But I
encourage you to do it anyway. Don't worry
about what anybody else thinks. Take the time
you need to grieve your loss.*
—Barbara G. Schmitz
*The Life of Christ,* 32

\* \* \*

*To you, O Lord, I lift up my soul; in you I trust,
O my God. Do not let me be put to shame.*
—Ps. 25:1-2

*G*rievers survive on the theme "one day at a time." Others use the tell-all phrase "so far so good." Now, however, the rigorous emotional and social agendas of the end of the year challenge that response. Holiday demands shove the griever into emotional overload. Decisions such as flight reservations, brunch reservations, and housing accommodations have to be made now. If the person decides to stay home during the holiday season, gifts have to be purchased or made, wrapped, and shipped, particularly if young children are the recipients.

Merchants force the issue. For some grievers, their first encounter with Christmas displays or merchandise—which gets earlier every year—produces angst: "Oh, no! How will I deal with *that!?*" Grievers who have been down this road advise: You will deal with it by making plans and by making backup plans. Some would advise, "Plan tentatively."

Some grievers and some families will decide "the holidays as usual" and go full steam ahead. Victor Parachin wisely counsels grievers to call a family conference in which everyone can express both needs and wishes. Realistically, "through compromise and negotiation everyone can get a little of what they really need." Unless you have someone who insists on having it "my way." That's when the skillful art of diplomacy begins.

✳ ✳ ✳

# APPRECIATE THE GRIEF STYLES AND DECISIONS OF OTHERS

*Keep in mind there has never been*
*a loss precisely like yours.*
—James E. Miller
*How Will I Get Through the Holidays?* 7

\* \* \*

*Please give me a loving heart that tries*
*to understand how other people feel.*
—Wendy Beckett
*A Child's Book of Prayer in Art,* 29

\* \* \*

*I did it my way.*
—Popular hit song of the 1980s

\* \* \*

*The eternal God is your refuge,*
*and underneath are the everlasting arms.*
—Deut. 33:27

*L*ook at your fingertips. No one on earth—no one—has a fingerprint like yours. So why should your *grief print* be predictable? You had a unique relationship with your loved one. Even if there were other siblings, for example, *your* sibling relationship was unique, slightly different than your brother or sister had with another brother or sister.

Some people are not comfortable expressing grief publicly. It's easy for those of us who are public with our grief to assume that individuals who don't outwardly show their emotions are not grieving. In fact, we may even assume that these individuals didn't truly love the deceased or didn't love as much as we did. It's like the movie in which superagent Jerry Maguire demanded, "Show me the money!" It's tempting to demand, "Show me your grief!" Men especially have been taught to "be strong" and to resort to the stiff upper lip and a snarled "I'm fine!"

Most families have the designated "strong one." Families whisper, "You have to be strong for [Name]'s sake." This is particularly true of male grief expression patterns: "Be strong!" or even more crassly, "Get a grip on yourself!" This restricts male grief expression. Some families have a "commentator" who does color commentary (like in professional sports) on every family member's grief. That can lead to additional tension during the holidays, especially if a family member insinuates, "I'm grieving *the most* [or *more* than you]." One expression of hospitality you can give others this holiday season is the gift of recognizing that grief has many formats and forms of expression.

✳ ✳ ✳

# ASK YOUR CHURCH FOR HELP

*Is any one of you in trouble? He should pray.*
*Is anyone happy? Let him sing songs of praise.*
*Is any one of you sick? He should call the elders*
*of the church to pray over him and anoint him*
*with oil in the name of the Lord. And the prayer*
*offered in faith will make the sick person well;*
*the Lord will raise him up.*
—James 5:13-15

\* \* \*

*Would it do violence to the scripture to suggest,*
*"Is any one of you grieving? He [or she] should*
*call the elders of the church to pray . . ."*

\* \* \*

*The Christian church is not a static institution.*
*It is men and women who flesh out in daily life*
*the meaning of faith, the reality of the risen Christ.*
—Myron S. Augsburger
in *Topical Encyclopedia of Living Quotations,* 31

$\mathcal{T}$he Church is made up of men and women who, instead of saying, "Been there, felt that!" lovingly pray, "Now, God, this child of Yours is grieving and needs Your help. How can I help?"

I grew up in a church that made up baskets for the needy at the holiday season. Most of the time it was foodstuffs and perhaps a ham or a turkey. We wanted everyone in our community to have a good dinner at least. As part of the "peace on earth, good will to men," we would care for those less fortunate. However, to my knowledge we never did anything specifically for the emotionally needy in our church or community. So some had full cupboards and refrigerators, presents around the tree, but empty hearts during the holiday season. We left them to get through the season the best way they could.

Don't hesitate to ask for prayer or seek time with your minister or perhaps a pastoral or grief counselor. The greatest task for the Church is to intercede for those who carry heavy spiritual and emotional burdens this season. Sometimes grievers expect the Church to be mind readers, but the reality is that these days many church leaders have not had a strong personal experience with death and grief—yet. So you may have to help them learn to be compassionately practical.

❊ ❊ ❊

# BE ALERT TO THE CULTURE'S OBSESSION WITH EXCITEMENT

*You can get lost in Christmas.*
—Julie Salamon
*The Christmas Tree, 7*

\* \* \*

*See to it that no one takes you captive through
hollow and deceptive philosophy, which depends upon
human tradition and the basic principles
of this world rather than on Christ.*
—Col. 2:8

\* \* \*

*Never apologize for choosing what will nurture you.*

\* \* \*

*Nineteen ninety-two is not a year I shall look
back on with undiluted pleasure. In the words
of one of my more sympathetic correspondents,
it has turned out to be an* "annus horribilis."
—Queen Elizabeth II of England, addressing Parliament
in *Bloomsbury Keys*, 235

\* \* \*

*Lord, it's _____.*
*How many years have I boasted about getting everything
ready, checking the list twice? I don't feel like celebrating
today. So come spend this day with me—because
I'm lonely, afraid. I don't want to spoil anyone else's
[Thanksgiving; Christmas; New Year's].*

*I*t's bad enough as a griever to hear, "I am soooooo excited!" It's the next part that wounds: "Aren't *you* excited?" Generally, the season fanatics want parties that have pizzazz, Christmas musicals and programs that dazzle, gifts that provoke speechlessness and an "I don't know what to say" response.

You want to scream, "Stifle yourself!" You just want—somehow—to get through the season without breaking down in a nine-tissue episode of public grief.

You'll hear "Joy to the World" in both traditional format and also in the upbeat version. The word "joy" will stick in your throat at times. The last thing you want to be called is a party pooper. You may suspect the accusation even when you don't hear it.

But seasonal excitement is not always soul deep. For many people, it's "Put on a happy face and at least act excited!" Some will even stretch the truth: "Fine. Thank you for asking. I'm just fine."

You can expect someone to do the lecture or mild-mannered pep talk: "It's been nine months since Harry died. You've got to get on with your life. Have some fun!" Every clichéd suggestion sounds as if it ends with an exclamation mark.

Yes, you'll be lonely during the holidays—but you won't be the loneliest. Some of the loneliest people this holiday season are those who sleep with a partner in a cold, dull bed; who perform perfunctorily in the gift exchange, emitting "Thanks!" dripping with sarcasm; who rely on a carefully negotiated script to get them through the family gathering.

Some activities may well be so excitement focused, you will want to politely "pass."

✳ ✳ ✳

27

# BEFRIEND YOUR GRIEF

*Fully engaging in mourning means that you*
*will be a different person from the one*
*you were before you began.*
—Anne Brener
*Mourning and Mitzvah*, 30

✳ ✳ ✳

*The LORD blessed the latter part*
*of Job's life more than the first.*
—Job 42:12

✳ ✳ ✳

*Permission to mourn granted.*
—Barbara Lazear Ascher
*Landscape Without Gravity*, 98

✳ ✳ ✳

*Don't let anyone take your grief away from you.*
*You deserve it, and you must have it. If you had a broken*
*leg, no one would criticize you for using crutches until*
*it was healed. If you had major surgery, no one would*
*pressure you to run in a marathon the next week.*
*Grief is a major wound.*
*It does not heal overnight. You must have the*
*time and the crutches until you heal.*
—Doug Manning
*Don't Take My Grief Away*, 65

This society has worked to eliminate many public symbols of grief. Once women wore black for a full year after a death. Mourning wreaths were hung on the door of the residence. The gold star in the front window announced a wartime casualty. These symbols warned individuals who might not know of the loss.

Grief—even during the holiday season—has important lessons to teach those who pay attention. Some have discovered that previous holiday traditions, celebrations, and expenditures must be reevaluated and altered. Others have come to appreciate the traditions even more. My friend Dennis Apple, after the death of his son, rethought the traditions of their last Christmas and wrote in his newsletter what may be permission for you this year: "Go ahead and do it!"

Some have learned that the season is not so much about giving as it is about relating. These holidays offer ample opportunity to treasure the memory of those we have lost—and to treasure relationships with those who are still with us.

Remember: you're not forever jettisoning seasonal happiness. This year, however, grief is a reality that must be recognized, appreciated, perhaps tolerated. Grieving must be included as something of a temperamental houseguest in the holiday plans and decisions.

One widow told me that every Christmas she had taken off work and spent the two days prior to the holiday frantically baking, cooking, decorating, and cleaning. But it felt good—if she could be honest, she said—to enjoy a fine meal in a restaurant and to invest the time she had previously spent in the kitchen in being with her children and grandchildren instead. And they loved being with Gran.

\* \* \*

# BEFUDDLE SOMEONE

*"I am very sorry, sir. I am behind my time."*
*"You are? Yes. I think you are.*
*Step this way, if you please."*
*"It's only once a year, sir. It shall not be repeated.*
*I was making rather merry yesterday, sir."*
*"Now, I'll tell you what, my friend. I am not going*
*to stand this sort of thing any longer.*
*And therefore," Scrooge continued,*
*leaping from his stool, and giving Bob*
*such a dig in the waistcoat that he*
*staggered back into the Tank again—*
*"and therefore I am about to raise your salary!"*
*Bob trembled, and got a little nearer to the ruler.*
*"A merry Christmas, Bob!" said Scrooge,*
*with an earnestness that could not be mistaken,*
*as he clapped him on the back.*
*"A merrier Christmas, Bob, my good fellow,*
*than I have given you for many a year!"*
—Charles Dickens
*A Christmas Carol,* 57-58

✳✳✳

*God, help me to have at least one moment,*
*however slight, to put aside my grief*
*to surprise someone this season.*

*I*t's easy for grieving people to seize Ebenezer Scrooge's line and bark or whimper, "Bah! Humbug!" to anyone and everyone during the last weeks of the year. Someone will offer a "Merry Christmas" that sends you over the edge and into a ferocious "What's so merry about Christmas?"

Grievers also have the right to befuddle—to surprise or delight another individual. Maybe you're in a position to play the postvisited Scrooge and be generous. During my first Christmas alone in California, one way I fought my loneliness was by throwing a Christmas cookie decorating party. Everyone decorated cookies and talked about holiday plans and traditions. The next day I called the Salvation Army to ask if they could use dozens of Christmas cookies.

"Sure—bring them down," I was told.

The commander, however, was stunned—no, befuddled—when he peeled back the box lids and discovered that the cookies had not been merely smeared with icing but had been individually, and in several cases elegantly, decorated. Needless to say, those cookies were a hit delight at the senior adult party sponsored by the Army.

A widow chose Christmas to befuddle her family by dispensing the large collection of nutcrackers her husband had collected across the years.

Befuddling puts into motion something that evolves into a story for years to come. "I remember the year he [she] . . ."

✳ ✳ ✳

# CAROLIZE YOUR SEASON

*O come, O Key of David, come*
*And open wide our heavenly home.*
*Make safe for us the heavenward road,*
*And bar the way to death's abode.*

*Rejoice! Rejoice! Emmanuel*
*Shall come to thee, O Israel!*
—Latin hymn, 12th century

\* \* \*

*Be near me, Lord Jesus; I ask Thee to stay*
*Close by me forever, and love me, I pray.*
*Bless all the dear children in Thy tender care,*
*And fit us for heaven, to live with Thee there.*
—John Thomas McFarland

\* \* \*

*Sing and make music in your heart to the Lord.*
—Eph. 5:19

*T*he carols can become a prayer for those moments when we simply cannot compose our own prayers.

I learned a great lesson from a widow named Eunice, who told me that after her husband's death she decided to live with "lots of lights, lots of color, and lots of good smells." I would add lots of sounds to her list (but not necessarily lots of volume). Music is a major ingredient in the holiday season. It's never too early for me to begin playing the seasonal music, particularly the carols.

Certainly some particular carols or holiday songs bring a flood of memories, even tears. But the carols also enliven. They become our sung hope. This may be the year to "sit with the carols" and really listen to their words. While Paul encouraged the Ephesian believers to sing, he added for our benefit, "and make music *in your heart*" (emphasis added). For some of us, this is not our year to sing aloud. But by listening attentively, we can make the music in our hearts that we can't get to cross our lips. By reading through a book of carols, you might stumble upon one of the lesser-known carols such as "Hark the Glad Sound! The Savior Comes." I discovered these wonderful words:

> *He comes the broken heart to bind,*
> *The bleeding soul to cure,*
> *And with the treasures of his grace*
> *To enrich the humble poor.*
> —*Christmas Carols, 9*

A particular seasonal song may capture your attention or become the "tidings of comfort and joy." That's become reality for me with the English carol "Once in Royal David's City." So make the decision "to prepare Him room" with lots of music. You may want to call a radio request line for a particular song to be played in memory of your loved one. You may leaf through the newspapers' entertainment or "Music of the Season" sections to identify for some places to hear good Christmas choral and instrumental music. Perhaps purchase some new tapes or compact discs if the old favorites make you uncomfortable.

# CELEBRATE SENSITIVELY

*Ask yourself what you really need this Christmas*
*to balance the rest of your life.*
—Jo Robinson and Jean Coppock Staeheli
*Unplug the Christmas Machine,* 63

\* \* \*

*Lord, this season reminds me that whenever I am weak,*
*You are strong. Is it all right if I grieve around You?*
*I have to act strong everywhere else. I need a place*
*just to be a griever, full of questions, full of tears at times,*
*overwhelmed by absence.*

\* \* \*

*Whether you eat or drink or whatever you do,*
*do it all for the glory of God.*
—1 Cor. 10:31

*I*f the death was recent, or if you are still exhausted, you may find yourself going overboard to work up the seasonal spirit. Especially in a culture that urges, "Spend! Spend! Spend!" You may be still uncertain of your new financial realities. Still, you may be tempted to have a "make it up to them for all they've been through" season. Some grievers have been financially and emotionally irresponsible, especially if they're trying to escape the reality of the loss. When someone opens a gift and exclaims, "You shouldn't have!" he or she might be right.

Sometimes in mid-holiday season grievers need something of a midcourse correction.

We need to remind ourselves—or have someone lovingly remind us—of our decision to celebrate sensitively.

# CONSIDER THE
# NEEDS OF EVERYONE

*Young children, of course, have great expectations
at Christmas, and they need to know that life continues,
even after the death of a loved one.*
—Helen Fitzgerald
*The Mourning Handbook,* 108

✳✳✳

*While grief in life is unavoidable, we do still have
a choice about how we respond to our feelings
and how we spend for our holidays.*
—Barbara Johnson, *Spatula* newsletter, undated

✳✳✳

*Women tend to feel this disappointment most acutely
because they are the Christmas Magicians, r
esponsible for transforming their families' everyday lives
into a beautiful festival. No matter how busy they are,
they bear the burden of pulling a magical celebration
out of the hat year after year.*
—Jo Robinson and Jean Coppock Staeheli,
*Unplug the Christmas Machine,* 22

✳✳✳

*Heavenly Father, God of all compassion, comfort us in
our sorrow following the death of [Name]. Let us find
hope in Your steadfast love; give us wisdom to face all the
challenges and circumstances of life with [Name]'s death.
In Jesus' name we pray. Amen.*

*I* remember how different Christmas felt that first year after my dad's death. From the ride home from my nephew's home where the clan had gathered to exchange presents, to the quiet Christmas morning breakfast with just me and my mother. Dad's absence seemed *especially present.* There was no one to tell us how the weather was going to be; Dad had always gotten up first to attend to that chore. Simple expressions like "Going to snow, weatherman says" echoed through my memories.

Unfortunately, we are so quick to deal with everyone's needs that we fail to include ourselves in "everyone." We do things, against our good judgment, so others will not be disappointed. Over time I've made the decision, as a single person, not to spend Christmas with my family. Initially my sister annually protested, "It won't be Christmas if you're not here!" but she has come to recognize my need for a quiet holiday.

When I sing, "I'll be home for Christmas," I mean at 404 East 81st Street. That's now *home.*

If someone asks, "Are you up to this?" be honest. This is not just humming "I did it *my* way!" or bruising the emotions of others for your own needs. But if you force yourself to do seasonal activities you don't want to do, you may inherit emotional consequences long into the new year. As a griever, honor your needs.

✻ ✻ ✻

# CREATE NEW TRADITIONS

*One thing you can do is start some new tradition
that is so different from old celebrations
that it has no painful memories for you.*
—Helen Fitzgerald
*The Mourning Handbook,* 110

\* \* \*

*And don't forget: the child you are exposing
to an old Christmas tradition may even be yourself.
If there is something you have always thought
you would like to do or see at Christmas,
make this the year to do it!*
—Jan Dargatz
*52 Simple Ways to Make Christmas Special,* 85

\* \* \*

*Creator of all, we thank You for the gift of life You
gave to [Name]. In our confusion and grief help us to
remember this season the joy that he [she] brought us.
Guide us through the choices and demands
about the traditions of this season. Amen.*

Traditions have great value, but not in all situations. Sometimes people keep them simply because it is too much trouble to be creative or innovative. Some traditions are more habit than meaningful expressions and are something of the path of least resistance. Not a few grieving families, after reflection, have discovered the old tradition has pretty well worn itself thin. The death or loss provided a way to terminate it.

Admittedly, lots of people sometimes do a radical shift without careful reflection. So the family who had always done ski Christmases found themselves emotionally and spiritually marooned on a warm, sunny Florida beach. Only no one would say, "Bad idea."

Traditions can be mothballed, recycled, or rekindled. You may need to give someone permission to create a new tradition. At least hear out their "What would you think if *this year* we . . . ?"

# CREATE ORNAMENTS OR DECORATIONS THAT SYMBOLIZE YOUR LOVED ONE AND ETERNAL LIFE

*It is Christmas that makes Easter possible;*
*it is Easter that makes Christmas possible.*
—Barbara G. Schmitz
*The Life of Christ,* 33

\* \* \*

*Those who live in the Lord never see*
*each other for the last time.*
—German motto
in *Topical Encyclopedia of Living Quotations,* 68

\* \* \*

*We do not want you to be ignorant about those who fall*
*asleep, or to grieve like the rest of men, who have no hope.*
*We believe that Jesus died and rose again and so we believe*
*that God will bring with Jesus those who have fallen*
*asleep in him. . . . For the Lord himself will come down*
*from heaven, with a loud command, with the voice of the*
*archangel and with the trumpet call of God, and the dead*
*in Christ will rise first. After that, we who are still alive and*
*are left will be caught up together with them in the clouds*
*to meet the Lord in the air. And so we will be with the Lord*
*forever. Therefore encourage each other with these words.*
—1 Thess. 4:13-14, 16-18

\* \* \*

*O Lord, Christmas and Easter have now*
*become linked in my heart through Jesus.*

*L*ook at the ornaments on a person's tree. Sometimes you can learn a lot about that person through them. So this year might be the year to creatively talk about what eternal life means and then find ways to find symbols to capture that reality. Certainly angels would be one easy-to-find ornament. You might want to use white ribbon, since white represents resurrection.

An ornament with the year of the deceased's death or span of years might be appropriate. Or you might invite family members to give some creative attention to making ornaments. You can find hollow, clear ornaments in craft stores that could be filled with symbols of the life of the deceased. Make opportunities for individuals to take a moment to explain their ornaments. Be sure to gather the family and friends around to hang those special ornaments on the tree.

And creating an ornament may give some a chance to capture feelings through symboling. My friend Roberta created wonderful ornaments honoring her brother and sent them to his friends at Christmas. On trees in Florida, Connecticut, and Missouri hung reminders of the fresh reality of eternal life.

# CRY IF YOU WANT TO

*Jesus began to weep.*
—John 11:35, NRSV

\* \* \*

*What soap is for the body, tears are for the soul.*
—Jewish proverb
*Leo Rosten's Treasury of Jewish Quotations,* 449

\* \* \*

*A sorrow that has no vent in tears*
*makes other organs weep.*
—Henry Maudsley, 18th-century physician
in *Mourning and Mitzvah,* 46

\* \* \*

*A great Jewish leader, Rabbi Tzvi Rabinowicz, reminds,*
*"It is . . . unnatural not to weep for the dead"*
—Kay, *A Jewish Book of Comfort,* 79

\* \* \*

*Jesus, help me to grieve well today. I seem to*
*be crying a lot. I always seem to be apologizing*
*for crying. My tears seem to make everyone uncomfortable.*
*But it's not as if I have an on-off switch. One minute I'm*
*fine; then, out of nowhere, like floodwaters ravaging a*
*small creek bed, the tears sweep over me. Can I at least*
*know that I can cry around You and not have to apologize?*

$O$ne of the great hit songs of several decades ago was "It's My Party," which included those words followed by "and I'll cry if I want to." Just substitute "grief" or "holiday" for "party," and you have a theme song that will empower you during the holidays. Tears will show up, perhaps, in the times you least expect them and perhaps not in the moments you do expect them. Or the tears may flow all the time.

Some people cannot handle tears. Immediately they scurry for the tissues. They may interrupt you with a tissue or a hankie, politely refraining from saying, "Stop crying." Even a mild "There, there!" may mean "Quit crying." That is how many grievers experience an offered tissue.

Tears are an eloquent expression of our loss. In Roman times, tears were captured in small vials and treasured. Now ours lay in wadded heaps of tissue in the bottom of wastebaskets.

You may want to schedule some times alone—so that you can cry freely. You may also need to be prepared for something of a sneak tear attack that leaves you wondering, "Where did that come from?" It could be a song your loved one enjoyed, a memory that chose this particular moment to ask, "What about me?"

Our grief is punctuated by sighs, tears, and sometimes groans. Remember: if someone is bothered by your tears, it's *his or her* problem. You may be polite, wave away the tissues, and still keep crying. That's a griever's choice. By crying, you might invite another to stop what he or she is doing and to "be with" you or to perhaps shed his or her own tears. During the holiday frenzy, you take a time-out for coffee. You take a time-out for a quick bite on the run. Do yourself a favor—take a time-out for tears as well.

✳ ✳ ✳

# DEFINE YOUR BOUNDARIES

*Take time to admire the poinsettias!*

\*\*\*

*"I want to minimize Christmas preparations."*
*"I want to feel more relaxed this holiday season."*
*"I want to simplify my gift giving."*
*"I want to spend more time with children*
*this Christmas."*
*"I want to* _____*."*

\*\*\*

*Lord, help me to define safe boundaries. Protect me from*
*the clichés, the easy answers, the tendency*
*of people to say, "If I were you . . ." Guard me from the*
*"oughts," the "shoulds," the "have tos."*
*Help me to grieve well this day, this season.*
*You gave me [Name] for all those years.*
*Help me not to dash through my grief. Give me strength to*
*do what, at that moment, I think I can't do. Surprise me*
*again today, with Your grace sufficient for my grief.*

*D*uring this emotional season, boundaries fall like trees in a forest filled with enthusiastic lumberjacks. Grievers get talked into buying stuff, eating stuff, attending stuff—and berate themselves for not saying, "No." So, early in the season, take a long look at your calendar. You might even want to block out some dates by writing "booked," followed by your initials. These blocked-out dates are for time alone, seasonal rest and relaxation.

The song says, "Dashing through the snow," but these December days most of us are dashing from social obligation to social obligation, with no time to stop to admire the poinsettias, to really taste the holiday treats, to savor the cappuccino, so to speak. We sidestep every "I wish you didn't have to rush off."

It will be easy for someone to talk you into doing something you will regret with an "I won't hear of you not going!" One griever decided, when she found the first Christmas catalog in the mail, "I'm giving gift certificates this year." With her checkbook she "did Christmas" in about 15 minutes. By avoiding the crowded malls, the fights for parking spaces, the lines, the noise, the fatigue, she invested in her own healing. (And no one complained about the certificates!)

You can expect someone to protest or challenge your decision: "Of course you're coming!" But if you've spent time reflecting on and determining your boundaries, they will be easier to maintain.

\*\*\*

# DO WHAT YOU NEED TO DO

*If there is one thing I have learned . . . it's that we all grieve
in our own ways and on our own schedule.*
—Candy Lightner
Founder of Mothers Against Drunk Driving
in *When a Loved One Dies*, 288

✳ ✳ ✳

*Because my son's birthday always fell very close to
Thanksgiving Day, we always had his birthday dinner on
his day [Thanksgiving]. Everybody knew his real [birthday]
dinner was the Thanksgiving meal. He always loved it.
. . . The first Thanksgiving after my son died, my husband,
my daughter, and I determined we wanted no part of
old traditions that day. . . . We steered clear of family
and friends and had dinner at the Benihana of Tokyo
restaurant. You can't get much further away from tradition
than that. But it was what we needed to do that year.*
—Mary Cleckley
"What a Difference a Year Made," 1

✳ ✳ ✳

*Jesus, you knew rejection and disappointment;
help us if our [celebrating] seems distasteful;
help us to decide what best to do,
what next to do, or what to do at all.*
*A New Zealand Prayer Book*, 130

*I*t is easy for grievers to end up doing things to please others during the holiday season. Whether it is "Oh, come on—just one more store, one more mall. . . . We won't stay long" or "Everyone will be *so* disappointed if you're not there." Going solo to a holiday event that you always attended as a couple can be emotionally draining. Your body may ache from the pent-up tension, from pretending that you are doing so well. One widow told me that her decision to go off on a cruise during Christmas was misunderstood—but she needed the time away to think, to reflect. Others, however, have booked cruises and found them to be emotional nightmares: "He's in a metal box in the ground, and I'm in a metal box [a cabin] on a cruise ship in the Caribbean."

So maybe it's the year for you not to do your Julia Child impression and cook and bake till you drop. Maybe this is the year you do not make everyone's favorite foods and desserts and fudge. Do what *you* need to do.

Postholiday seasonal fatigue is a reality for many adults; for the griever, a full season on the circuit of parties and shopping and eating can be emotionally sabotaging. In fact, it can compound grief. Do only what you need to do.

✳ ✳ ✳

# DONATE TO YOUR CHURCH OR A CHARITY IN HONOR OF YOUR LOVED ONE

*Do not withhold good from those who deserve it,*
*when it is in your power to act.*
—Prov. 3:27

\* \* \*

*Common acts of tzedakah [act done in memory*
*of a deceased loved one] include projects undertaken,*
*volunteer time committed, books donated, financial*
*contributions made to projects and organizations*
*which the deceased supported in*
*life. . . . The main thing is to feel that your*
*tzedakah reflects the values of the deceased,*
*continues your relationship with him or her,*
*and is consistent with your own values.*
—Anne Brener
*Mourning and Mitzvah, 184*

$\mathcal{M}$any churches decorate for the holidays with poinsettias to memorialize loved ones. So that may be the first step to honor your loved one(s) in your faith community. And you may decide to contribute to some of the charities and causes your loved one was committed to. You may want to send a donation to a medical foundation researching the disease your loved one died of. On the memo line of the check write, "In memory of [Name], the greatest [friend, son, daughter, wife, husband, or so on] in the world."

Sometimes when I drop a contribution into a Salvation Army kettle, I do it to honor Bud, Martin, or Paul, who always responded generously to the Salvation Army's Christmas appeals.

Your contribution does not have to be cash. You could do some volunteer work as well.

✳ ✳ ✳

# DO NOT FAST-FORWARD TO JANUARY 5

*My grace is sufficient for you,*
*for my power is made perfect in weakness.*
—2 Cor. 12:9, RSV

\* \* \*

*Day by day, and with each passing moment,*
*Strength I find to meet my trials here.*
*Trusting in my Father's wise bestowment,*
*I've no cause for worry or for fear.*
*He whose heart is kind beyond all measure*
*Gives unto each day what He deems best,*
*Lovingly its part of pain and pleasure,*
*Mingling toil with peace and rest.*
—Caroline V. Sandell-Berg

\* \* \*

*Sometimes the only way through it—is through it.*

\* \* \*

*Not somehow, but triumphantly!*
—Bertha Munro

*I*t may be tempting to do a seasonal hibernation and mutter, "Wake me up when it's all over." Many grievers have remarked at the start of this season, "I wish I could go to bed and wake up in mid-January." Indeed, some use numbing instruments such as alcohol, food, shopping, being constantly on the go, to do just that.

Kris Kristofferson sang, "Help me make it through the night." Grievers may well sing, "Help me make it through *the holidays.*"

But the holidays have serendipity moments—those wonderful emotional and spiritual ambushes, moments when joy sneaks up on you. In the midst of great grief, there are small moments that break through to our hearts. We need those to buffer our souls and spirits for the tough times. It may begin with a simple prayer: *Lord, help me make it through **this** day.* It may end with a simple offering of gratitude: *Lord, thank You for helping me make it through this day.*

Millie, a widow, had it right. When people asked how she was making it without Herb, who had been called "Mr. Christmas," she answered, "One day at a time." Sometimes that translates "one *hour* at a time."

\*\*\*

# FORGIVE THOSE YOU BELIEVE ARE RESPONSIBLE FOR THE DEATH

*Lord Jesus Christ, I ask today for Your help that I may
forgive everyone in my life who has hurt me. I know that
You will give me strength to forgive. . . .
Lord Jesus, I especially pray for the grace of forgiveness
for that ONE PERSON who has hurt me most.
I ask to forgive anyone whom I consider
my greatest enemy, the one who is the hardest
to forgive or the one whom I said I would never forgive.
Thank You, Jesus, that Your will is to free me
from the evil of unforgiveness.*
—Anonymous prayer
in *How to Pray When Life Hurts,* 34, 36-37

\* \* \*

*Be kind and compassionate to one another,
forgiving each other, just as in Christ God forgave you.*
—Eph. 4:32

\* \* \*

*Forgiving is for giving.*

$\mathcal{R}$oy Lawrence has had long experience as a person of prayer and a teacher of prayer. To one woman he taught what he called "forgiveness praying." Each day she would specifically forgive someone—until she ran out of people to forgive. Moreover, she was to follow up her prayer by doing a practical act to show that her forgiveness was real —such as writing a letter, making a phone call, offering a gift, trying to restore a broken relationship.

Some people cannot get to the work of grief because they are so busy reciting and rehashing the injustices, slights, and failures of people, some of which are unforgivable if not unforgettable.

Sometimes the griever must make the first move in restoring the injury.

Consider giving generous gifts of forgiveness—to yourself for not visiting the nursing home more often, for being too sharp in criticizing other family members who you believe failed to pull their weight. Forgive those who offer faux pas statements that hurt more than soothe. Forgive your loved one for not taking the doctor's advice.

Forgive God for "taking" your loved one.

✳ ✳ ✳

# GIVE YOUR GRIEF ITS VOICE

*My mind is so disturbed . . . that I can scarcely write,*
*in short my dear friend my heart is nearly broke.*
—Andrew Jackson to John Coffee
22 December 1828 immediately after Rachel Jackson's death
Meacham, Jon. (2008). *American lion: Andrew Jackson in the White House.*
New York: Random House, p. 6

\* \* \*

*O my God, I cry out by day, but you do not answer,*
*by night, and am not silent.*
—Ps. 22:2

\* \* \*

*Oh, my anguish, my anguish! I writhe in pain.*
*Oh, the agony of my heart! My heart pounds*
*within me, I cannot keep silent.*
—Jer. 4:19

\* \* \*

*Jesus, You know what it is to be speechless in grief.*
*When Your friend Lazarus died, You made no long*
*speeches. You wept. Eloquently You expressed Your grief.*
*Help me find my voice to put my grief into words.*

*S*ome people squelch their grief. Some grievers work like lion tamers, ferociously snapping their whip to keep the lions (words and emotions) in the cage: "If I let my guard down for even a moment . . ." By putting down the whip, you might take a gigantic leap toward healing.

It might be through notes to family members and friends, some of which you may mail; others you may not mail. Notes or letters can be read at the grave or scattering ground of your loved one.

You could give your grief its voice by including it in your cards or in your Christmas newsletter. Be honest.

Don't sugarcoat your loss. You could give your grief its voice by taking a moment around the table or the tree, to speak a word about your loved one.

Giving your grief its voice makes it easier for others who are with you or around you to give their grief its voice. Many don't want to bring it up but will welcome you, saying, "It's OK to talk about [Name]." And it is OK for your voice to be punctuated by pauses and silences and tears.

\* \* \*

# GIVE YOURSELF PERMISSION TO SAY, "NO," OR "I'LL PASS"

*"I don't want to hurt her feelings . . ."*
*Oh, but you're willing to hurt your own feelings!*
*"See, Elizabeth, we have to be whatever we are at any*
*given time in our lives, even when we are wounded.*
*We have to live that moment on the*
*way to other moments."*
—Armand DiMele
in *Seven Choices: Taking the Steps to New Life After Losing Someone You Love,* by
Elizabeth Harper Neeld, 96. Copyright © 1990 by Neeld & Neeld, Inc. Reprinted
by permission of Clarkson N. Potter, a division of Crown Permissions, Inc.

\* \* \*

*Lord, I do not want to spend an evening around happy,*
*happy people. I do not want to sit here*
*around me either. Give me the courage to say,*
*"I'll pass, but thank you for inviting me."*

*N*obody knows your grief better than you. Nobody knows if you are up to a social event better than you. You have had the experience of missing an event and hearing, "You didn't miss much" as well as "Oh, you should have been there."

Sometimes, the best way to take care of yourself as a griever is to say, "No," or "I'll pass." Sometimes being home in comfortable clothes, listening to music, and nursing a mug of spiced tea or eggnog may do your soul more good than attending or making small talk at a party or open house—or listening endlessly to the holiday plans or a rehashing of the mall antics of others.

But remember that ordinary events have a way of becoming extraordinary. Jesus performed His first miracle at a wedding reception by turning water into wine. This invitation might be an opportunity for Jesus to turn your grief into a something less than sorrow.

# GUARD YOUR HEART

*The man who comforts a beautiful young widow*
*does not only intend to perform a good deed.*
—Jewish proverb
in *Leo Rosten's Treasury of Jewish Quotations*, 478

\* \* \*

*I loved him before I ever saw him. He was searching for*
*something, and so was I. Our lives miraculously intersected*
*like two comets hurling in our own orbits of great need.*
*I was (unhappily) single. He was (unhappily) married.*
*He said he was getting a divorce . . . "soon."*
*I (naively) believed him.*
—Lisa Hudson
"That's Just the Way Grief Is," 12

\* \* \*

*So, if you think you are standing firm, be careful that you*
*don't fall! No temptation has seized you [or will seize you]*
*except what is common to man. And God is faithful;*
*he will not let you be tempted beyond what you can bear.*
*But when you are tempted, he will also*
*provide a way out so that you*
*can stand up under it.*
—1 Cor. 10:12-13

*M*any grievers don't realize how emotionally and romantically vulnerable they may be after the death of a spouse, especially after a long illness, and physical and sexual intimacy has been missing in the relationship. It's easy for friendly relationships to become romantic or quasi-romantic. Some individuals are what I call "emergency room technicians"—"I know just what you need: some tender loving care." Naturally, then, *that* individual volunteers to provide the TLC. And *that* individual probably knows where the mistletoe is hanging.

A premature social relationship is a dangerous numbing element that confuses children of any age and that actually interferes with or intrudes on your grief—moreover, everyone's. You may protest, "Oh, he makes me feel so alive again." Certainly there is nothing wrong with feeling alive. But you need to ask one question: "What am I pretending *not* to know about this relationship?"

Too many grievers have complicated their grief and created new grief by jumping into emotional and sexual relationships. Romance can be a pleasant distraction from the realities of grief, particularly during this triathlon of holidays. (But the big one comes six weeks into the new year: Valentine's Day.)

Give yourself plenty of time. Guard your heart.

✳ ✳ ✳

# INVITE GOD'S HELP

*Into your hands I commit my spirit.*
—Ps. 31:5

\*\*\*

**God is closest to those with broken hearts.**
—Jewish proverb
in *Leo Rosten's Treasury of Jewish Quotations,* 237

\*\*\*

**Jesus, help me grieve well. You gave me [Name]
for all these years. Help me not to dash through
my grief. Heal my heart. Give me strength to do
what I think at the moment I cannot do!
Give me wisdom this holy season.
Surprise me again with Your enabling grace.**

The theme of this generation could well be "I did it my way." Some people will just hunker down and somehow get through the season. But God wants to help you. Ask. Simply, some of the most honest prayers of the season will be little more than, *O Lord . . .* Many grievers, through previous losses, have learned to ask specifically, *Help me get through **this** party [or **this** open house]. Help me get _____ done.*

The old hymn "Yield Not to Temptation" is not a Christmas tune, but Horatio R. Palmer must have understood something of grief:

> *Ask the Savior to help you,*
> *Comfort, strengthen, and keep you.*
> *He is willing to aid you;*
> *He will carry you through.*

With help comes gratitude: *Thank You, Lord. I couldn't have made it through this day [this week, this holiday] without Your help.* After all, as Palmer noted,

> *Each vict'ry will help you*
> *Some other to win.*

✳ ✳ ✳

# JOURNAL YOUR GRIEF

*A journal is not only a record of events that touch and transform us; it is a private space in which we can meet ourselves in relation to others and God.*

—Susan A. Muto
*Pathways of Spiritual Living,* 94-95

✳✳✳

*Sometimes we need a jump start to get us writing. Try one of these:*
- *When I think of Christmas without you, I feel . . .*
- *I remember the Christmas we [you] . . .*
- *The best gift you ever gave me was . . .*
- *The thing I'll miss most this Christmas is . . .*

✳✳✳

*Insights that are hazy figures on our horizon sometimes become crystal clear when committed to a journal.*

—Richard Foster
*Freedom of Simplicity,* 109

✳✳✳

*A journal is something of a book of remembrances, a personal Ebenezer to say, "Hitherto the Lord has helped us" (1 Sam. 7:12 [RSV]).*

—Richard Foster
*Freedom of Simplicity,* 108

Thoughts about the holidays often resemble something of the bumper cars at the county or state fair. You are enjoying the ride, minding your own business, when Bam! you get rammed. So it will be with memories and ideas competing for your attention. "I'm not telling you what to do, but you should do this. . . . You *ought to* [do, think, buy, cook, plan] . . ."

Some grievers have badly bitten tongues by the middle of December. Trying to keep from saying things they want to say to some insensitive or seasonally pushy person or persons. One helpful practice for many grievers has been to retreat to their journals.

I encourage grievers to spew, to sit down and begin writing and not to move until three pages are full. Forget about punctuation, spelling, or who might see your words and thoughts. Just get the thoughts, words, and fears down on paper. Amazingly, some of them lose a lot of their wallop by being corralled on paper.

It can be a delicious feeling to reread your words, and say, "Whew! Glad I got that out of my system!"

Or you may want to write more meditatively. Begin by saying, "God, would You be with me in this time as I journal? Would You bring me clarity about . . . ?" or "What should I do about . . . ?" Or use this to jump-start your writing: "What bugs me the most about the holidays this year is . . ."

Always date and time the writing. Down the emotional road, you will want to go back and reread what you wrote. You may be able to look back and see how God worked specifically in resolving the issue. And journaling offers you perspective on how far you have come on the grief journey.

\* \* \*

# KEEP THE FUTURE IN MIND

*How long must I wrestle with my thoughts and
every day have sorrow in my heart?*
—Ps. 13:2

\* \* \*

*"I know the plans I have for you," declares the LORD,
"plans to prosper you and not to harm you,
plans to give you hope and a future."*
—Jer. 29:11

\* \* \*

*The best thing about the future is that it
comes only one day at a time.*
—Abraham Lincoln

\* \* \*

*An Eastern monarch once charged his wise men to invent
him a sentence to be ever in view, and which should be true
and appropriate in all times and situations. They presented
him the words: "And this, too, shall pass away." How much
it expressed! How chastening in the hour of pride! How
consoling in the depths of affliction!*
—Abraham Lincoln
in *Familiar Quotations,* 521

\* \* \*

*It has taken me many months to get to the point where
I can say, "All right, the future is not going to be what you
thought it was. It's gone, and you're not going to have it.
You just will not have it. Your future went with him.
Now you've got to build a new one."*
—Unidentified widow
in *Seven Choices: Taking the Steps to New Life After Losing Someone You Love,* by
Elizabeth Harper Neeld, 71. Copyright © 1990 by Neeld & Neeld, Inc. Reprinted
by permission of Clarkson N. Potter, a division of Crown Permissions, Inc.

*I*s every holiday going to feel like this? I'm young." The son wanted an answer and a reprieve from his first holiday without his father. Just as Abraham Lincoln, you, too, may discover that some of the most hope-packed words in the English language may well be "This, too, shall pass." The wisest advice I can offer to grievers is "Never say 'never,'" as in "I will *never* get over this," or "I will *never* have a good Christmas as long as I live."

A young widow was told, "You are young—you'll remarry!" by a houseguest. Initially she didn't respond. But in a thank-you note she wrote, "You were close to us so many times. There is one thing you must know. I consider that my life is over, and I will spend the rest of it waiting for it really to be over."

Jackie Kennedy wrote those words in January 1964, fewer than 60 days after her husband's assassination and days after her first holiday as a single mother. Yet she rebuilt her life as a mother and a successful book editor. Indeed, she had a future of 30 years.

I would urge you to memorize Jer. 29:11. Put it on your refrigerator, in your checkbook, on your computer screen.

God is always actively involved in creating a future and a hope for each of us.

# LET OTHERS IN ON YOUR GRIEF

*If you find that hope eludes you and the future stretches
before you dark and bleak, then you can ask another
person to hold your hope for you, and to believe in you
even when you have difficulty believing in yourself.
Then their hope can sustain your hope.*
—James E. Miller
*How Will I Get Through the Holidays?* 55

\* \* \*

*Praise be to the God and Father of our Lord Jesus Christ,
the Father of compassion and the God of all comfort,
who comforts us in all our troubles, so that we
can comfort those in any trouble with the
comfort we ourselves have received from God.*
—2 Cor. 1:3-4

\* \* \*

*God, do You see what's happening to me?
Can You help me?*

\* \* \*

*The people who have helped me are not those
who have answered my confessions with advice,
exhortation or doctrine, but rather those who have listened
to me in silence, and then told me of their own personal
life, their own difficulties and experiences.
It is this give and take that
makes the dialogue.*
—Paul Tournier
*The Meaning of Persons,* 191

*S*ome individuals are quick to pull up the drawbridge over the moat and isolate themselves in their grief. Some will not return phone calls or E-mail messages or make commitments. Have you placed a Do Not Disturb sign on your heart? Do you dismiss invitations with an "I'll get back to you"? Are you so focused on grief's being personal that any inquiry is viewed as an intrusion? Fortunately, despite your stiff upper lip and "No Trespassing" routines, people continue to knock.

Others have been down the grief path. You're not the first person to wrestle with Christmas seasonal grief. What other grievers have learned firsthand may be insightful to you. Let people in on your grief. Consider them something of grief consultants. Let them help you put up decorations or accompany you to the cemetery or the mall. Ignore the temptation to mimic an independent-minded three-year-old and to declare, "I can do it myself."

Spend some time listing things that people could help you do to make it through this season. Then when they ask, simply respond, "Could you help me decorate?" or "Could you go shopping with me Tuesday evening?" I doubt that Joseph had a line of credit for his relocation from Nazareth to Bethlehem, let alone Egypt. I believe the wise men had a secondary function: to finance Joseph's flight. Joseph did not turn down the gifts offered by the visitors from the East. He let them in on the great unfolding drama. Do yourself and your family a favor: Let someone in on your grief.

✳✳✳

# MAKE GRATITUDE

*It was Thanksgiving. A joke of a holiday.*
—Elizabeth Harper Neeld
on her first Thanksgiving as a widow

*Seven Choices: Taking the Steps to New Life After Losing Someone You Love,* by
Elizabeth Harper Neeld, 63. Copyright © 1990 by Neeld & Neeld, Inc. Reprinted
by permission of Clarkson N. Potter, a division of Crown Permissions, Inc.

\* \* \*

*Our challenge this Thanksgiving morning is to see*
*our lives the same way, to learn how to give thanks*
*at this altar for not only the mixed blessings of Christ's life,*
*but also for our own, to say "thank you" for the*
*whole mess, the things we welcome as well as the*
*things we would risk our souls to escape.*
—Barbara Taylor
*Mixed Blessings,* 43

\* \* \*

*Lord, according to the calendar,*
*according to the merchants,*
*it's Thanksgiving.*
*A day to deliberately give thanks!*
*But "Thanks for what?" is what comes to my mind.*
*For death? For thick grief that suffocates my joy?*
*All I can think about*
*is how silent my world is*
*without [Name].*
*I cannot be grateful on my own.*
*I cannot psych myself to sing,*
*"We gather together to ask the Lord's blessings . . ."*
*You are going to have to help me.*
*Help me be grateful, at least,*
*for all the good memories of the years*
*I shared this day with [Name].*

*M*ost people think our leadoff celebration of Thanksgiving traces back to the Pilgrims giving thanks at Plymouth Rock. Hardly. In the years after the founding of this nation, festivities were rather sporadic until Sarah Josepha Hale, a widow with four children, launched a crusade for a formal national day of thanksgiving. By hand, each year, Mrs. Hale wrote letters to every president and every governor. Her persistent requests for a national day were ignored, until in the aftermath of the decisive Union victory at Gettysburg, President Lincoln wanted some national day of tribute. The Secretary of State, William Seward, remembered the persistent annual letters he had received as governor of New York. On Seward's advice, on October 3, 1863, President Lincoln declared that the last Thursday in November would be a national day of thanksgiving. After Lincoln's death, Sarah Hale lobbied for Congress to enact the legislation rather than rely on a president proclamation.

One persistent, letter-writing widow gave this nation Thanksgiving. One widow committed to making gratitude may well be something of a patron saint to grievers today.

Take time this day to deliberately state or write your gratitudes.

Today I am grateful for _____.

\* \* \*

# MINIMIZE THE
# SEASONAL STRESSORS

*Grief can't be shared. Everyone carries it alone,*
*his own burden, his own way.*
—Anne Morrow Lindbergh
in *Camp's Unfamiliar Quotations,* 124

\* \* \*

*As Jesus and his disciples were on their way,*
*he came to a village where a woman named Martha*
*opened her home to him. She had a sister called Mary,*
*who sat at the Lord's feet listening to what he said.*
*But Martha was distracted by all the preparations*
*that had to be made. She came to him and asked,*
*"Lord, don't you care that my sister has left me*
*to do the work by myself? Tell her to help me!"*
*"Martha, Martha," the Lord answered, "you are worried*
*and upset about many things, but only one thing*
*is needed. Mary has chosen what is better,*
*and it will not be taken away from her."*
—Luke 10:38-42

\* \* \*

*Do you really enjoy all the rituals that*
*have become second nature to you at Christmas,*
*or have they become habits?*
—Jo Robinson
*Unplug the Christmas Machine,* 64

*E*veryone has asked at some point in the holiday season, "Why am I doing this?" Actually we need to ask that about everything we do that is part of this season. Sure, some people love the details of a party, lavish sit-down dinners, a ski trip, or the decorating and scheming to really surprise someone. But it often takes a holiday partner to make everything happen. Now, your loved one's death means only one person to make it happen this year.

Some grievers merely roll up their sleeves and groan, "If it's to be, it's up to *me*." One widow decided to skip the Christmas cards. Initially she wondered, "What will people think?" But someone reminded her that she had just mailed all the funeral and kindness thank-you notes. "That's sufficient *this* year." By not doing the particular event, you are not forever canceling the tradition. Just think of it as a sabbatical.

✳ ✳ ✳

# MISS THE INVITATIONS TO PARTIES AND OTHER SOCIAL EVENTS

*The sooner every party breaks up the better.*
—Jane Austin
in *Bloomsbury Keys,* 195

✳✳✳

*Do we have a right to distract ourselves from our pain with our joy? Do we have a right to happiness, those of us who are walking scars? Do we have a right to joy? To the future? I remember those questions. I asked them too.*
—Anne Brener
*Mourning and Mitzvah,* 40

*I* didn't want to go to her stupid old party anyway!"

Admittedly, some invitations will not come this year. It will not be an oversight. Ever since the ark was unloaded, people have been thinking socially in twos, fours, sixes. It is, in many ways, a couple's world still. Some hostesses or planners may assume you are emotionally unpredictable: "What if she would break down and start crying over the pâté and cold cuts?" Some may fear you will cast a dark shadow across the festivities. Moreover, "out of sight, out of mind" is a reality in denial.

If I do not have to see you or sense your grief at the party, social, and so on, then I can create my own reality. Because if I see a grieving parent at a seasonal event, I look into a mirror and realize, "There but for the grace of God go I." Certainly the loss of the invitation will hurt. Yes, the social distancing, especially if it is awkward, will hurt, even wound. But attending or trying to fit in the seasonal joviality of others may have frustrated you or possibly wounded you.

75

# NAP

*To do nothing is the most difficult thing in the world—*
*the most difficult and the most intellectual.*
—Oscar Wilde
in *Camp's Unfamiliar Quotations*, 146

\* \* \*

*He [Elijah] came to a broom tree, sat down under it and*
*prayed that he might die. "I have had enough, LORD,"*
*he said. "Take my life; I am no better*
*than my ancestors." Then he lay down*
*under the tree and fell asleep.*
—1 Kings 19:4-5

\* \* \*

*O Lord, in the course of this busy life, and now this*
*bereavement, give us times of refreshment and peace;*
*relief from all the demands; and grant that we may*
*so use our leisure and rest to rebuild our bodies*
*and renew our minds, that our spirits may be*
*opened to the goodness of your creation;*
*and that we may be reminded of your*
*faithfulness to us;*
*through Jesus Christ our Lord.*
—adapted from *Book of Common Prayer*, 825

$\mathcal{T}$ired, exhausted people complicate the holidays for others, if not also for themselves. A nap can be a wonderful gift to yourself. It is easy for some grievers, with long "to do" lists, to say, "Who has time to nap?" The accurate response may be: Do yourself—and the world—a big favor: take a nap.

\* \* \*

# NETWORK WITH OTHER GRIEVERS

*No man is an Island, entire of it self; every man
is a piece of the Continent, a part of the main.*
—John Donne

\* \* \*

*The one who suffers alone suffers most.*
—Jewish proverb
in *Leo Rosten's Treasury of Jewish Quotations*, 440

\* \* \*

*If one falls down, his friend
can help him up. But pity the man
who falls and has no one to help him up!* . . .
*Though one may be overpowered,
two can defend themselves.
A cord of three strands
is not quickly broken.*
—Eccles. 4:10, 12

*A*ll grievers need *Mehom Hanekhama,* a safe place to grieve. Unfortunately, that may not be within a family, or within a circle of friends, or even within a church. Those who try to do their grief work in isolation are closeted in many ways. Grievers need places to take questions, wonderings, and to discover that other grievers have, or have had, those same questions.

It may lead to great relief: "You mean I'm not crazy?" one widow said with a sigh.

"No, Honey," one wise group member remarked. "You're just grieving."

By becoming involved in an organized network or support group of grievers, you can discover—

- You are not alone.
- Some people can be trusted with your thoughts and wonderings.
- The experience of another griever may have some raw resources for your healing and grief journey.
- Honest expression of emotions is healthy.
- Mourning is not an illness or self-indulgence of a bad habit.
- The season strategies that work for others

"Every griever has three needs: (1) to find the words for the loss; (2) to say the words out loud; and (3) to know the words have been heard," says Victoria Alexander in *Words I Never Thought to Speak,* ix.

Often, only the support group provides a safe enough place for the griever to accomplish all three needs. In such a setting, the griever rarely needs a translator. And it just may be that your words jumpstart the words in the heart of another griever.

✻ ✻ ✻

# NURTURE YOURSELF

*A little neglect may breed great mischief. . . .*
*For want of a nail the shoe was lost;*
*for want of a shoe the horse was lost;*
*and for want of a horse the rider was lost.*
—Benjamin Franklin
in *Camp's Unfamiliar Quotations*, 215

\* \* \*

*God our Creator, our center, our friend, we thank you for*
*our good life, for those who are dear to us, for our dead,*
*and for all who have helped and influenced us. We thank*
*you for the measure of freedom we have, and the extent to*
*which we control our lives; and most of all we thank you*
*for the faith that is in us, for our awareness of you and our*
*hope in you. Keep us, we pray you, thankful and hopeful*
*and useful until our lives shall end. Amen.*
—*A New Zealand Prayer Book*, 183

*I*f you were caretaker for your loved one and have been through a prolonged dying process, you may be physically, emotionally, and spiritually drained before the Christmas season even begins. Maybe you have not had time enough to rebound from all the demands of grieving. For some the holiday demands become the final straw.

Perhaps you have been so busy caring for other family members in their grief that you have ignored your own needs. Or you may have been embroiled in legal and financial responsibilities in settling or untangling an estate. You may be compromising your own future health by not taking care of yourself. McDonald's has it right: "You deserve a break today." Whether it's a long hot soak, a massage, a day at a health spa, or simply checking into a hotel for a day of quiet and reflection, be good—to yourself.

List three ways you could nurture yourself this holiday season:

1.

2.

3.

✳ ✳ ✳

# OBSERVE A QUIET HOLY DAY

*In all your ways acknowledge him.*
—Prov. 3:6

✳✳✳

*We are so afraid of silence that we chase ourselves from
one event to the next in order not to have to spend
a moment alone with ourselves, in order not
to have to look at ourselves in the mirror.*
—Dietrich Bonhoeffer
*Meditating on the Word,* 60

✳✳✳

*On this first Thanksgiving, Christmas, or New Year's Eve
without your loved one, give yourself permission to take
a time-out from all the clamor of the season.
Give yourself a gift: some moments of silence.
Then at the end of the holiday, raise your right hand
over your left shoulder and give yourself a pat
on the back. You made it through!*

*C*onsider the definition of "quiet" for all the members of the family, especially the children.

Only a slight difference exists between two words: quiet and quite. In postholiday commentary, some will say, "We had *quite* the holiday!" while others will lament, "Quite the holidays!" when the credit card bills start appearing. However, this may be your year for a quiet holiday after a long series of "quite!" holidays, each one bigger than the last.

Quiet holidays can be healing. One family found it wonderful not to do the frantic drive-11-hours mad dash to the grandparents, but to spend the time in their own home, their own beds, and their own bathrooms. Holidays without the beehive of frantic frenzy provide generous time to pay attention to each other.

One family had made the decision after their son's death to spend Thanksgiving on a "getaway" vacation. Then one day before the trip the mother found her young daughter crying. She learned that at school the daughter had heard all of her friends talking excitedly about their family's plans and had even made decorations for the table. "Not only is Eric dead, but we're not even having a Thanksgiving dinner! And there's no place for my turkey [her decoration]." Quickly the mother reassessed the family's plans for an on-the-road trip.

As the family sat at the table quietly after the father said grace, the ten-year-old said she had something to add: "I want to thank Mommy and Daddy for making this very special dinner for our family. And most of all, I want to thank you, God, for having let us have my brother Eric for six years."

—Harriet Schiff
in "Sibling Grief," 3

\* \* \*

# ORGANIZE YOUR LIVING ENVIRONMENT

*Sit down! Hush up!*
*Stop trying to fix things!*
*Be still for a while.*
—Lois Wagner, RN

Wagner, Lois. Cited in Palmer, Anita. (2005 Summer). Writing the last chapter: PLNU school of nursing professor advises tackling end-of-life issues now. *Viewpoint*, 3-5.

✳ ✳ ✳

*This place, O Lord, now seems so silent without [Name]. This home has become a house, loneliness is so evident. All the exuberant enthusiasm of youth has been sucked from these walls. Lord, all those times I hassled him about the messiness of his room, I wish I could take them back! The silence at night reminds me of the too many times I ordered him to turn down the music.*
*I wish, Jesus, that I had asked him.*

*D*uring a prolonged illness, housecleaning may be limited to the most necessary tasks. Now, with the seasonal demands on you, who feels like cleaning? And then having to clean again after the holidays are over. Indeed, many of us are so busy that we have learned to accept lite housecleaning.

A good top-to-bottom housecleaning could be a joint family holiday project, or, if you dare, a task for those who volunteered, "Let me know if there's anything I can do to help."

Break up monumental (or what seem monumental) undertakings into smaller, more manageable segments. Do something every day to organize your environment.

Note: If you have houseguests or family members who check behind the refrigerator, this is not the year to invite them for the holidays.

✳ ✳ ✳

# PREPARE

*Let ev'ry heart prepare Him room.*
—Isaac Watts

\* \* \*

*No matter how difficult it is, we must learn to carve
some holes in our schedules, some moments of
study and prayer and spiritual nourishment beyond what
happens in church, or else we will find ourselves with
precious few tools to work with when it comes to
growing ourselves or our homes.*

*[Reflecting on her experience of breaking a leg
before Christmas] But when you spend that much time
at home, you think about home a lot.*

*And on one of those cold days, while waiting
for Christmas to come and the crutches to go,
I realized that the Lord was right. I knew how
to make a home for him. And that most of us do.*

*I am slowly coming to understand that if we know how
to make a place for those who need rest and quiet,
a place where people can recover from the hustle
and bustle of the world and its wounds,
then we can make a place for the Lord.*

—Peggy Benson

*Listening for a God Who Whispers: A Woman's Discovery of Quiet Understanding,*
54, 90-91. Copyright 1991 by Peggy Benson. Reprinted 1994 by Vaughan Printing
and Solitude and Celebration Press. Used by permission.

*C*hristmas always costs something—but it costs more not to celebrate." I wrote those words a decade ago for *The Gifts of Christmas,* but I believe in them as much this holiday season. Death has altered my tradition and celebration, or at least the participants in my traditions. The rigors of writing two doctoral dissertations were a subtle temptation to skip Christmas. That, however, would have impoverished me.

I'm concerned about grievers who will somehow, someway, get it all done by the big day. By "it" I mean the items on their lists. But should "prepare Him room" be at the top of their lists, especially this year, when sorrow casts its dark shadow across their space? At some point the thought will cross their minds: "Oh, yeah—Christmas is a religious event." But it will be mute. What God wants to whisper is, "It could be so much more, if you would prepare room for Me."

You may not be tempted to overspend.

You may not be tempted to overeat.

You may not be tempted to dowse your loss with drugs or alcohol.

You may, from sheer exhaustion, from anger, from one too many demands, not hear the knock of the coming Guest. You may, in words uttered by an innkeeper those centuries ago, say, "No room; I have no room." Some this year will growl: "Go away!" Others may choose to be polite. But the reality is the same: there's no room unless you prepare it!

✳ ✳ ✳

# READ

*Some books are to be tasted,*
*others to be swallowed,*
*and a few to be digested.*
—Francis Bacon
in *Familiar Quotations,* 181

*A* good book is a welcome companion for grievers. You might browse a bookstore or library for seasonal stories for all ages. You might find a collection of holiday readings, one for each day. Even if you live alone, read them aloud. If you need to pause, pause. Savor a line, a phrase, a word, a hope. Here are some of my favorites for the Christmas coffee table and bedside:

*The Invisible String,* by Patrice Karst

*Kneeling in Bethlehem,* by Ann Weems

*A Cup of Christmas Tea,* by Tom Hegg. A story for all of us "just too busy" to sit with an older relative or friend for some cookies, conversation, and a cup of tea.

*The Christmas Miracle of Jonathan Toomey,* by Susan Wojciechowski. An incredible story of a single parent asking a widower woodworker to make a Nativity set.

*The Nativity,* illustrated by Julie Vivas. The traditional story captured in pictures that will bring a smile to your face.

*A Christmas Carol,* by Charles Dickens

*The Gift of the Magi,* by O. Henry

*A Christmas Memory* and *The Thanksgiving Visitor,* by Truman Capote

Read the Christmas narratives. Relive the dramatic unfolding of the Christmas event. If you're not up to reading, ask a child or a grandchild to read to you or with you.

If you're traveling to spend Christmas with others, make room in your luggage for one children's book. Reading that book to a child or hearing it read by a child could be a wonderful jump-start for you. If you can't imagine reading, remember that there are incredible colorful gift books with a minimum of words.

✳ ✳ ✳

# REMAIN OPEN TO
# SEASONAL SURPRISES

*One morning as I sipped a cup of coffee while I was
on the phone talking with an editor in New York,
I looked out the picture window and saw a baby deer
walk gingerly by, sniffing at the pink geraniums.
It paused, framed against the pink granite dome of the
capitol of Texas in the distance. Here it was, God's world
and my new world laid out before my eyes.
"I'll have to call you back," I hastily told the editor.
"I've got to take this in."
And I sat there for five full minutes gazing at the wonder
of it all, reflecting that I had just learned how to move from
loneliness to solitude. There is a vast difference.*

—Liz Carpenter

in *Seven Choices: Taking the Steps to New Life After Losing Someone You Love*, by
Elizabeth Harper Neeld, 124. Copyright © 1990 by Neeld & Neeld, Inc. Reprinted
by permission of Clarkson N. Potter, a division of Crown Permissions, Inc.

✵✵✵

*This season tell someone, "I'll have to call you back.
I've got to take this in."*

✵✵✵

*Because of the Lord's great love we are not consumed,
for his compassions never fail. They are new every
morning; great is your faithfulness.*

—Lam. 3:22-23

✵✵✵

*Open my eyes, that I may see
Glimpses of truth Thou hast for me.*

—Clara H. Scott

✵✵✵

*Sneak up on me today, Lord.
Keep me open to Your surprises.*

$\mathcal{B}$e interruptible this season. Sometimes grief cleanses the soul, and it's amazing what we can see. That's why I love the Christmas song "Do You Hear What I Hear?" Simply change the verbs:

Do you *see* what I see?

Do you *feel* what I feel?

Do you *smell* what I smell?

By remaining open to surprise, you might see a child wrestle with the decision to save her quarter or to drop it into a Salvation Army kettle—and begin a long tradition.

By remaining open to surprise, you might see the wonder of a man finding just the right present for the woman he loves, the last one in her size.

By remaining open to surprise, you might hear a new word or sentence in a Christmas or other seasonal song that will echo through the canyons of your heart for years to come.

By remaining open to surprise, you might really "taste" a Christmas goody all the way to your soul.

By being surprisable, someone might wish you a "Merry Christmas!" that will resound and send hope waves flooding your heart.

By being surprisable, you just might hear the angels sing.

\* \* \*

# REMEMBER REALISTICALLY

*My soul is downcast within me;*
*therefore I will remember you.*
—Ps. 42:6

✳ ✳ ✳

*How can we sing the songs of the LORD*
*while in a foreign land?*
—Ps. 137:4

✳ ✳ ✳

*I'm convinced the reason we are here is to remember, if we*
*understand memory to be that uniquely human ability to*
*create from the past a sense of meaning in the present and*
*a trembling anticipation of possibility for the future.*
—Student to Elizabeth Harper Neeld
after the death of Neeld's husband

in *Seven Choices: Taking the Steps to New Life After Losing Someone You Love,* by
Elizabeth Harper Neeld, 226. Copyright © 1990 by Neeld & Neeld, Inc. Reprinted
by permission of Clarkson N. Potter, a division of Crown Permissions, Inc.

✳ ✳ ✳

*Lord, I find myself wanting to forget—to forget that it is*
*Christmas again. This one I have had time to anticipate.*
*But I really do not want to remember happier holidays.*
*I do not want to remember. But I do want to remember*
*all the ways You have stood with me.*

*I*t's a little gimmick motivational speakers use to illustrate concentration: "For the next six minutes, don't even think of peppermint ice cream! Just put it out of your mind." By just suggesting the ice cream delight, some say, "Yeah—right!" You may not have thought about peppermint ice cream since last Christmas, but it is now on your mind.

The same principle applies to the holidays. Do not say the name. Do not even think about the deceased's favorite holiday foods. Just don't . . . Particularly, just do not think of sexual warmth and cuddling of Christmases past. Just put it right out of your mind.

Grievers who get into emotional trouble are those who are trying so desperately, so rigidly *not* to think of the person. Do yourself a big emotional and spiritual favor: remember. The Jewish people, in bondage in a foreign land, were asked to provide entertainment for their captors by singing some of the songs they were known for. The Jewish people were repulsed. "How can we sing at a time like this?" You might read this passage, "How can we sing the songs of the season while in a foreign land called 'Grief'?" But the psalmist followed this verse by noting the severe consequences in forgetting Jerusalem.

But you may also need to remember the other realities of the loved one—the years your gift effort produced only a grunt or a one-star "thank you." Balanced remembrances are necessary so that we have realistic recollections. It's what the Jewish people call *hesped,* or balanced memories. It is easy under the guise of "speaking no ill of the dead" to turn the loved one into something he or she was not. By weighing the remembrances, the scales might come out that a majority of the seasons were good. Focus on that reality.

\*\*\*

# RESIST THE TEMPTATION
# TO MAKE IT UP TO OTHERS
# FOR WHAT THEY'VE
# BEEN THROUGH

*In a moment, I think you'll agree with me: having more cash makes the holidays happier. Call a caterer and give yourself and your friends a really wonderful holiday party. Or splurge on a gift someone will never forget. . . . You've got the kind of spending power that's bound to give the happiest of holidays to those who mean so much to you.*
—Letter from credit card company, November 1997

*G*ive the gift of yourself. And as at a big family dinner, it's OK to ask, "Does anyone want seconds?"

Splurge. Spend. "A gift someone will never forget." It will be tempting this season after all you have been through, particularly if death followed a long illness, to want to celebrate not just by a wonderful party but by a *really* wonderful party.

Gifts can be just another method to numb, to distract from the pain of your loss.

You cannot make it up to anyone. If anything, this death has me more aware that what you value is not stuff, but people, relationships. Maybe it is the fact that Scrooge, after coming to his holiday senses, sent the biggest bird in London to Bob Cratchit. Does that settle the debt? Does that erase all the seasons when the Cratchits celebrated with the smallest bird?

If you want to be gracious, give a large hunk of yourself.

Say "no" to the suggestion—or rather the temptation—that you can make it up to them.

And you can expect that someone will go overboard in gifts to you as if it could douse your heightened sense of loss this season.

\* \* \*

# RETHINK YOUR HOLIDAY SHOPPING HABITS

*Too many people spend money they
haven't earned, to buy things they don't want,
to impress people they don't like.*
—Will Rogers

\* \* \*

*A mall, at Christmastime, can be a
most unfriendly place to a griever.*

\* \* \*

*Santa Claus has become the patron saint of malls.*

\* \* \*

*For some grievers, the mere thought of holiday gift
shopping brings on great distress and anxiety. . . .
Some alternative ways to shop this season include
phone orders, catalog-based purchases,
or shopping early in the season before the
stores are filled with holiday shoppers
[or even before the decorations go up].*
—Victor Parachin
"What to Do When the Holidays Hurt," 50

\* \* \*

*This day, O Lord, be with me in all I do.
Give me clarity in buying, shopping, giving.*

The intricate plans Gen. Dwight D. Eisenhower of the United States drafted for the invasion of Europe pale compared to the plans many have for the days between the turkey and the final minute of the last bowl game. The Christmas song reminds us of ecstasy: "as the shoppers rush home with their treasures" or what, at the time, seemed like treasures. Or what they hope the recipient will consider a treasure. But, after a certain point in the rush of the season, to get the treasure, you may have to fight for it.

Crowded malls and scarce parking spaces are unhealthful for grievers—especially if you team Christmas shopped before with your loved one. You had a designated "uh-huher" (even vetoer) and package carrier. If you're determined to shop, decide to shop during off hours or early mornings. Know exactly what you're looking for, rather than wandering from store to store. You may find it helpful to recruit a "mall buddy" to accompany you for emotional support as well as those moments when you need someone to ask, "What do you think?"

While shopping can be a momentary respite from the grief, it may only heighten your irritability or restlessness, especially if you have a list of requests a mile long. Some grievers wisely have decided to buy only the necessary gifts—particularly if there are young children. This may be the year for gift certificates or checks. Some have decided to use Christmas as a time to transfer family heirlooms or emotionally laden belongings of the deceased.

Without planning your shopping, you could end up bitterly berating yourself for hasty, "this will have to do" gifts.

✳ ✳ ✳

# SAY YOUR LOVED ONE'S NAME

*I will give them an everlasting name*
*that will not be cut off.*
—Isa. 56:5

\* \* \*

*Lord, I'm learning that people, family, friends get*
*very uncomfortable whenever I say [Name]'s name.*
*Some have gasped. Some have frowned. Some*
*have looked stunned. A few have walked away.*
*But, Lord, my loved one had—or is it "has"?—a name.*
*Why should I stop saying it? May I say it*
*during the time I spend with You?*

\* \* \*

*Consciously remembering those who have died*
*is the key that opens our hearts, that allows us*
*to love them in new ways.*
*As we remember what we love about those who*
*have died, we welcome them back into our lives*
*even though we are apart.*
Attig, Thomas. (2000). *The heart of grief: Death and the search for*
*lasting love.* New York: Oxford University Press, p. 27

*S*oon after a person dies, family, friends, and associates start "pronouning." They say, "*He* died," rather than "David died." It is amazing how many grievers themselves pronoun their loved ones, saying, "*She* died," rather than "Carol died." The conspiracy of silence suggests that, no matter how awkward, whatever you do—do not say the name. As a griever you have the right to challenge pronouning.

Deliberately say the name—"*David* loved Christmas," or "Oh, how *Mary* enjoyed watching the bowl games!" Your intentionality will make it easier for others to say the name as well.

You'll set an example they will remember when their turn to grieve comes.

✳ ✳ ✳

# TOAST YOUR LOVED ONE

*Whatever you do, don't say his name.*
—Advice given to guests before a Christmas meal

\* \* \*

*Consider beginning your Christmas dinner*
*[or other gathering] with a special ritual to remind you*
*of why you are all together. It can be as simple as a prayer,*
*a toast, a candle-lighting ceremony,*
*or just a few quiet moments holding hands.*
—Jo Robinson and Jean Coppock Staeheli
*Unplug the Christmas Machine*, 135

*I* would like to propose a toast to the memory of _____, who this year spends Christmas in the real world."

Let those around the table respond, "May his or her memory to us be a blessing."

Rather than working feverishly to avoid saying the name, it is healthier to take the opposite approach and to deliberately find a time in the holiday gathering to specifically mention the name. Just before opening the presents, or at the dinner table before dessert, might be the time to say, "We're going to go around and share one characteristic of [Name] you appreciated. Or share your favorite memory." Remember: the sharing may start a little bumpily. In fact, you might want to ask someone ahead of time to break the ice with an "I'll go first."

Admittedly, with some of our loved ones there will be negatives as well. As noted earlier, the Jewish faith talks about *hesped,* the honest balancing of the good and the bad memories of the deceased. Close the time with a moment of silence or prayer. Or you might say or ask someone to say, "I would like to propose a toast to the memory of [Name]."

You only compound your grief by deciding not to mention the deceased, not recalling his or her contributions to the family's memories and traditions.

✳ ✳ ✳

# TRY

*The epitaph on the grave of Rev. Ralph David Abernathy:*
*"He tried."*

∗∗∗

*Every new thing that happened,*
*I thought I would die! But I didn't!*
—a griever named Judy

∗∗∗

*No one is inviting you to be the life of the party.*
*They are merely inviting you to attend.*

∗∗∗

*You gain strength, courage, and confidence by every*
*experience in which you stop to look fear in the face [and]*
*you are able to say, "I lived through this horror.*
*I can take the next thing that comes along."*
*You must do the thing you think you cannot do!*
—Eleanor Roosevelt
Roosevelt, Eleanor. (1960). *You learn by living: Eleven keys for a more fulfilling life.*
Louisville, KY: Westminster/John Knox Press, pp. 29-30

*I* do not think I can do this." There will be many moments this season when that sentence will dash through your mind or across your lips. While dressing, minutes before an event, quiz yourself: "How will I ever get through this dinner [reception, party, or so on]?" Consider trying. Some grievers choose to go to events late and leave early. "Stay as long as you're comfortable" is advice offered by one grieving daughter. Drop-in events may be easier.

More than once grievers have decided simply to put in an appearance and have found comfort in a mutual commitment with someone else who says, "Now we will not stay long. Just let me know when you are ready to go."

✳ ✳ ✳

# UNPLUG THE CHRISTMAS MANIA

*Come, Thou long-expected Jesus,*
*Born to set Thy people free.*
*From our fears and sins release us;*
*Let us find our rest in Thee. . . .*

*By Thine own eternal Spirit,*
*Rule in all our hearts alone.*
*By Thine all-sufficient merit,*
*Raise us to Thy glorious throne.*
—Charles Wesley

\*\*\*

*Lord, how do I this Christmas find rest?*
*In years past, Christmas always seemed to race by;*
*this Christmas it drags by, in slow motion.*
*The moment I think, "Good—I've gotten my crying done*
*for the day," something stimulates an exiting of fresh tears.*
*The tiniest memory can bring the biggest gush of crying.*
*Oh, I can sing, "Let us find our rest in Thee," but it's*
*so hard to find that rest. I have to sort through all*
*my grief for the slightest molecule of rest. And just*
*when I think I have my grief tidied up, it multiplies.*
*Jesus, You were born to set Your people free. Can*
*You give me an "early release" from all this grief?*
*Lord, help me this Christmas to find the rest You promise.*

*O*ver the last years, many grievers have been deeply impacted and empowered by *Unplug the Christmas Machine*. That book encourages readers to determine healthful holiday plans, agendas, and priorities. Some of us have long felt we're on a treadmill that keeps speeding up. We wish we could find a way to tame the season.

So the Myerses are not having an open house this year. Before you say, "Good—a night at home," you learn that the Hendersons are having a dinner party for the office staff.

Grief offers us a reason to unplug the mania of the season, to redetermine that *this* is important, *this* is essential, *this* is optional. It becomes something of a Christmas audit. Perhaps over the years you've said some yeses (or even caved in) to a spouse's holiday desires and expectations. Now is the time to say, "Now that it is up to me (or somewhat up to me), what do I want this season to be?"

Some grievers initially feel guilty altering some seasonal practice. But were you really fully committed to that particular tradition in the first place? Some grievers allow their decision making to be governed by this question: "What would [the deceased] want me [us] to do?" It's OK to consider the question, but the decisions must be based on what will be helpful for the living.

# USE SOME OF YOUR SEASONAL DECORATIONS

*This may not be the year to decorate
from front door to sidewalk!*

\* \* \*

*You may decide to set up a photograph
(or photographs) of your deceased loved one
with some greens or bright-colored balls around it.
It will be as if your loved one was sharing the
holiday with you. However, since this can be
painful to others in your family who do not
find it as comforting as you do, check this out
on the others. You may have to find a place for
remembrance in a less obvious spot in your home.*
—Helen Fitzgerald
*The Mourning Handbook,* 108

\* \* \*

*Remember: You are not Martha Stewart!
And more than likely, she's not coming
to your house this season.*

\* \* \*

*Create a personalized centerpiece honoring the deceased.
Gather things that belonged to him or her—and arrange
them casually in the middle of the table instead of a floral
centerpiece. It is a gift to your guests and is a creative way
to include those who once dined at this table.*

*I* am not going to decorate!" I hear that commonly in my grief groups, particularly just before the holiday season. "Too many memories." In some cases, the deceased may have been the decorator. The deceased lit the house from top to bottom and was always concocting new ideas for Christmas decorations. Deciding not to decorate is like deciding not to mention his or her name. Memories of previous Christmas decorations will come to mind. So maybe it's time to use some of the ornaments and not go all out. Decorate casually.

Jean's husband had always put up, decorated, and taken down the tree. So she decided to have Thanksgiving dinner at her house (rather than the traditional Christmas dinner). She asked her grown children and their spouses to decorate. It worked beautifully. Jean's decision brought a richness of colors, lights, and scents into a home where a long slow dying had taken place. Jean has decided to continue the new annual tradition. She chose a smaller, artificial tree rather than a live tree and has begun distributing to each child ornaments that had graced the family trees across the years.

Also, consider asking the children or grandchildren to draw or create pictures to capture their understanding of the loss. Place those on doors and on the refrigerator.

Remember the people who said, "Just let me know if there's anything I can do." Cash in those coupons now! Ask individuals to help you decorate or take down decorations.

# VISIT THE CEMETERY OR SCATTERING GROUND DURING THE HOLIDAYS

*It's good—not morbid or macabre—for Christians
to visit the cemetery, especially in November. Remember
that the Bible tells us: God planted a garden and made our
first parents from the dust of the earth. Adam and Eve's sin
exiled them from Eden, and ever since then, human beings
have longed for the garden of paradise. His saving passion
completed, Jesus was buried in a garden,
forever making graves and graveyards holy places.
And when Magdalene spotted the Risen Lord
at dawn, she thought he was the gardener!
The cemetery reminds us of the Bible's gardens.*
—Prayers of Those Who Mourn, 48

\* \* \*

*After the Sabbath, at dawn on the first day
of the week, Mary Magdalene and
the other Mary went to look at the tomb.*
—Matt. 28:1

\* \* \*

*All we go down to the dust;
and weeping over the grave,
we make our song: Alleluia, alleluia, alleluia.*
—Contakion of the Departed, from the Orthodox liturgy

$\mathcal{H}$onoring the final resting-places of our loved ones is a major element of healthy grief. Admittedly, distance or other factors limit some grievers from visiting as often as they wish the cemeteries or the places where they have scattered the ashes of their loved ones.

During this season, place holiday decorations on the grave: a wreath, a small artificial tree, fresh flowers, or place a holiday card inside a baggie. Be creative. Read a passage from the Christmas story, sing a Christmas carol, share your seasonal plans, or simply share the silence.

Ask someone to accompany you to the cemetery. Someone may wish to drive you or ride with you but choose not to accompany you to the actual grave. Consider inviting another griever, and visit the graves of each other's loved ones.

# VOLUNTEER AT A
# SOCIAL SERVICE AGENCY

*The people who come [to a social service agency]*
*for food and shelter will touch your heart and get*
*on your nerves. Hey, they're only human. Like you.*
*If you withhold judgment—condemn no one and*
*put no one on a pedestal, even in the silence*
*of your heart—you will gain wisdom and*
*insight you never thought to possess. You will.*
—Mitch Finley
*101 Ways to Nourish Your Soul,* 88

\* \* \*

*Whatever your hand finds to do,*
*do it with all your might.*
—Eccles. 9:10

\* \* \*

*Thankfulness is a perfecting training for watchfulness.*
*One who sees the past's blessings*
*sees also the present's answers and*
*the future's opportunities.*
—Ken Gire
*Windows of the Soul,* 188

*I*t is possible to be so focused on grief that you lose touch with what is going on around you. One family decided to spend their holiday mornings volunteering at a soup kitchen. They had talked about doing this for years—but the first year without Ken, Marilyn called a facility and asked if they needed volunteers. After discussing the idea with the family, she called back and said, "You can count on us."

Marilyn had her doubts and devised something of a backup plan. But from their comfortable economic vantage point, this grieving family met individuals whose Christmas would have been bleak without the center's hospitality. Late that night her 16-year-old knocked on the bedroom door, came in, and sat on the side of the bed. "Mom, this was an incredible day. Dad would have been so proud of us."

You may not choose to volunteer for Christmas Eve or Christmas Day or New Year's Day. But it takes lots of preparation before the big meal to feed hundreds of people. Call and see when you can help.

✻ ✻ ✻

# VOTE YOUR CHOICES

*I've discovered that every new thing I do is
like a little grain of sand. I add one
grain of sand to another. It's beginning to feel
as if at some point they will form
one big block of granite that I can stand on.*
—Elizabeth Harper Neeld
in *Seven Choices: Taking the Steps to New Life After Losing Someone You Love,* by
Elizabeth Harper Neeld, 197. Copyright © 1990 by Neeld & Neeld, Inc. Reprinted
by permission of Clarkson N. Potter, a division of Crown Permissions, Inc.

✳ ✳ ✳

*One thing I do: Forgetting what is behind
and straining toward what is ahead,
I press on toward the goal.*
—Phil. 3:13-14

✳ ✳ ✳

*We find that trying to do it all and have it all and
be it all won't work. Because there's no time.
No time for "choose to do's" because the
"have to do's" and the red-tape and
the responsibilities swallow up the
time allotment of every day.*
—Richard Eyre
*Spiritual Serendipity,* 33

*D*o I celebrate today? One woman grieving her 20-year-old son disclosed that she made it through her long season of grief by voting.

"Every morning as I lay in bed, I voted: Am I going to face this day? Or am I going to pull the covers up over my head and stay *here?*" Most days, she admitted, she voted to get up.

Her suggestion is a good one. When you first awaken, ask yourself: Am I going to celebrate today? Or am I going to try to ignore the season? But what about tomorrow? Tomorrow is tomorrow. Today I will deal only with *today*.

But what if today goes badly? Tomorrow before you vote, remind yourself that yesterday is yesterday—past tense.

# WATCH CHILDREN

*Jesus called the children to him and said, "Let the little children come to me, and do not hinder them, for the kingdom of God belongs to such as these."*
—Luke 18:16

✳✳✳

*We were putting up the Christmas tree lights—
this had always been a job for Lee and the boys—
and they wanted me to hurry and turn the lights on.
So we turned off all the other lights in the house
and just had the tree lights on. The three of us
were sitting there in the living room looking at them,
and Jeremy spoke up and said, "Oh, Mama,
this is so nice. This is so nice. If Daddy were here,
he'd love it 'cause he always liked the lights.
This would be even happier if Daddy was here."
And I held him and said, "You're right, Jeremy.
We wish he was here, but he's not. And we'll just
have Christmas anyway. And it's all right for
us to remember how happy it used to be."*
—Widow

*S*ome children are confused. Their friends are excited about the season, and yet things can be very sad at home. Children have the ability to blend their grief in with the normal activities of childhood, however. Do not assume the child is not grieving or that he or she does not understand. Do not expect children to grieve like an adult.

Children have great wisdom to bring to holiday grief. A child may well have a life lesson for you.

If you have lost a child or adolescent, these holidays will be troublesome. I have never forgotten a woman whose baby had died. Sitting in our grief group, she pulled a "Baby's First Christmas" ornament from her handbag and demanded, "What am I supposed to do with *this?*"

We sat in silence until a man who had lost twins—one the day before Christmas, the other the day after Christmas—responded, "You put it on the tree, lady. That's what we did."

You may need to limit the time you are around other people's children, even children in the family. The reality is that the first Christmas led to a massacre of male babies in Bethlehem after Herod ordered their execution (Matt. 2:16-18). Parents who have lost babies have always had a tough time with the holidays.

# WATCH THE NUMBERS

*A question for the season: Are you
stuffing your face or stuffing your grief?*

\*\*\*

*Wine is a mocker and beer a brawler;
whoever is led astray by them is not wise.*

—Prov. 20:1

*A number* is any substance or behavior grievers use to distract from their feelings.

The holiday season can be continuous temptation for many. You can count on some new fabulous recipe that's "to die for." (It's amazing how people who have not experienced a close loss use "death" vocabulary.) I remember the first Christmas after my dad died, my mom baked all of her specialties. It gave her something to do. When I came home to spend a week, I numbed myself by gorging on sweets. I wish I could tell you that we talked about my father. No—we ate. You know the line, "Eat something—you will feel better." At times it was almost a continuous plate-to-mouth experience. I kept trying to swallow my grief! I even had talks with myself about how I needed to cut back on all the eating. Still, I *stuffed and numbed.* Guess what January and February were like: diets!

It is easy to judge those who numb their pain with alcohol or drugs. However, who condemns the fudge eater, the cookie devourer, the brittle muncher? Needless to say, I only complicated my grief by the constant sugar highs of the holiday.

✳ ✳ ✳

# WEIGH ANY CRITICISM OF YOUR HOLIDAY DECISIONS

*Contemporary society minimizes the appropriateness of grief. Even when the importance of mourning is recognized, the outside world imposes many distractions and demands. . . . With so many variables involved, it seems clear that the chronology of grief is unique to each person; this must be respected and never judged.*

—Anne Brener
*Mourning and Mitzvah,* 30

\* \* \*

*Come to my defense, O God. They're trying to tell me how to grieve. Tell them to leave me alone.*

—Ann Weems
After the death of her 21-year-old son
*Psalms of Lament,* 91

\* \* \*

*When all we are and everything we do are called into question, grant us dignity and direction, grant us patience; Jesus, be there then.*

—The Anglican Church in Aotearoa, New Zealand and Polynesia.
(1989). *A New Zealand Prayerbook.*
San Francisco, CA: HarperSan Francisco, p. 583

*S*ome of us have grown up or live in families that value opinion formation. That is why we fight over the tree, decorations, or how much to spend on Aunt Roberta's gift. Granted, we ask, "What do you think?" but some of us edit what we think to conform to what we *think* someone wants us to think.

Expect some criticism or at least commentary on your grief style and on the holiday decisions you make. Something is bound to annoy or confuse someone in your family or extended social network. A family gathering may be the occasion for you to detect and deflect criticism. A chance overhearing of a slice of commentary or a re-accounting of that commentary may wound you or provoke a "How dare you!" Sometimes criticism is based on ignorance or lack of perspective.

The critic has probably never been in your shoes—he or she has never had to make the decisions you have had to make or must now make. It sounds simplistic, but sometimes you simply have to ignore the criticism. You may have to have a conversation with your children—whatever their ages—to explain another's criticism or to re-explain your decision. That is another reason the family conference early in the season is so helpful—it not only gives an opportunity to plan but also helps bring clarity and some sense of consensus on holiday plans and decisions. It also means that some other family members can defuse the criticism before it reaches outlandish/wounding proportions.

✳ ✳ ✳

# WORSHIP

*It doesn't seem like Christmas Eve to me
unless there's a dad under the tree, muttering over
a set of pliers and instructions in the middle
of the night. So, the last few years I have ended up
sleeping on the couch or in Jetta Beth's bed
at Robert's [my son's] house.
But just before I do, I go to church. . . . I think it
may well be because I know that if I get to
Robert's too soon, I will have to work on the toys.
It may also be because it is beginning to feel like
it isn't Christmas Eve unless I go to church.*
—Peggy Benson

*Listening for a God Who Whispers: A Woman's Discovery of Quiet Understanding,*
161-62. Copyright 1991 by Peggy Benson. Reprinted 1994 by Vaughan Printing
and Solitude and Celebration Press. Used by permission.

\* \* \*

*O come, let us adore Him!
O come, let us adore Him!
O come, let us adore Him—
Christ, the Lord!*
—John F. Wade

$\mathcal{O}$ne of the great joys of the Christmas season is the opportunities for worship. During my dad's last Christmas hospitalization, I slipped away from the hospital late Christmas Eve afternoon for a 4 P.M. service in a church a block from the hospital. Apparently it had once been a large congregation; now there were 12 of us in a huge sanctuary. Still, singing the carols and hearing the words of Scripture became a sacred enabling moment for me, a spiritual oasis.

One difficult challenge you may face is what to do about church services. One widow reminded me, "That's where I miss him most—at church. All those years, same section of pews . . . and I miss his arm around my shoulders."

This could be the Christmas to sample Christmas through the eyes of another denomination or a different branch of Christianity. It may be quite "different," but consider it a learning, stretching experience. Remember the doctrinal creed: one Lord.

Look for a compact disc or tape of "Lessons and Carols" (my favorite is King's College, Cambridge), taped in one of the great cathedrals of England. The service is a sequence of readings from the Old Testament (such as Gen. 3, Isa. 9), the Nativity narratives, interspersed with the singing of traditional hymns that foretell the birth of Jesus. The services are often broadcast live on public radio.

By deliberately and intentionally attending worship experiences, you just might be in one of those settings where God whispers. He often does that when his people gather.

✻ ✻ ✻

# WRITE A YEAR-END LETTER TO YOUR DECEASED LOVED ONE

*Giving ourselves time to heal and creating space for
the process allows the painful memories to be replaced
gradually by more pleasant ones. The pain subsides,
and one remembers the whole relationship,
not just the most recent memories of illness and death.
We make peace with what was unresolved.*

—Anne Brener
*Mourning and Mitzvah,* 148

\* \* \*

*Lord, there are things I need to say, to put on paper.
Lord, there are things that are becoming radioactive.
Lord, there are things I need to remember.
Give me strength.
Let it be the real me—a griever—
who remembers, who writes.*

*L*ots of "stuff" in grief never gets resolved. It's like food in plastic bags in a deep freezer—waiting, perhaps, someday to be thawed. The year-end letter to a deceased loved one gives you an opportunity to "defrost" emotions and feelings. On paper thoughts, words, even accusation can become less destructive. Memories can become softer. I urge grievers to write the letter, keep it for a day or so, then burn the letter in the fireplace on New Year's Eve. Some have taken snippings from their tree, pieces of Christmas wrap, and then "let go" of those words.

Here are some sample topics to jump-start your letter:

*When I think about Christmases with you, I especially remember . . .*

*In losing you I feel that I have lost . . .*

*I wish you could be here to help me this season with . . .*

*I'm grateful for . . .*

*The thing I feel most guilty about when I think of you is . . .*

*What I don't miss about holidays with you is . . .*

*What I miss the most about you is . . .*

*One season tradition that I changed is . . .*

Include family members in the project. Children may draw a picture to capture their thoughts. You can place these in a holiday box under the tree until you dispose of it.

You may choose to "share" portions of the letter with family members, either individually or in a group. Or you could place a journal where family members and friends can write in it throughout the season. Some of us simply are not good at verbalizing, and others of us are not good at listening all the way to the end of a sentence. This process offers a place to "get it off our chests."

✳ ✳ ✳

# "YES" INVITATIONS THAT FEEL RIGHT

*Never start a sentence with "I should have . . ."*
Billboard in North Carolina

\* \* \*

*Movement can only happen when you begin to assume
responsibility for yourself and say "I won't" instead of
"I can't." You may say "I won't" because
of some very good reasons, but to say
"I can't" is to play the role of victim.*
—Doug Manning
*Don't Take My Grief Away,* 114

\* \* \*

*Lord, I am not asking You for a great,
exuberantly joyous day—just a day
a little bit better than yesterday.
Help me walk a step closer to healing today.*

$\mathcal{T}$he holidays are overrun with invitations. For some, there are not enough nights and days in the season to schedule all the activities. Some people feel required to say yes to all invitations, especially not to disappoint someone. Some invitations, say from the boss, are something of command performances: You *will* show up!

Admittedly, some understanding friends will give you the option of saying no: "I know this is a difficult time for you, and we'd really like you to come, but we'll understand." Those who have not had a firsthand experience with grief, however, may not be as sensitive.

If you are a recent widow or widower, at times you may feel like a fifth wheel or the party pooper. If you do not decorate, elaborate decorations in someone else's home may ignite your self-indictment: "I didn't even decorate." Listening to the joviality may be upsetting. Going out at night alone or coming into an empty residence may be unsettling.

So ponder the invitation. What are your options? What would you *like* to do? Think before you commit. And never second-guess rethinking at the last moment, either to go or not to go.

So if the invitation *feels* right, accept. If something nags you about the invitation, "No" is a good, self-nurturing answer.

✳ ✳ ✳

# "ZESTIZE" YOUR SEASON

*There are times when you need to take a break
from mourning and bring Shabbat's [the Sabbath's]
sense of renewal and restoration to your
daily experience of mourning.*
—Anne Brener
*Mourning and Mitzvah,* 51

✳✳✳

*On Shabbat, it is as if the mourner is not a mourner.*
—Rabban Gamaliel, first-century Jewish leader

✳✳✳

*David, wearing a linen ephod, danced before the* LORD
*with all his might, while he and the entire house of Israel
brought up the ark of the* LORD *with shouts and the sound
of trumpets. As the ark of the* LORD *was entering the City
of David, Michal daughter of Saul watched from a window.
And when she saw King David leaping and dancing before
the* LORD*, she despised him in her heart.*
—2 Sam. 6:14-16

*M*aybe you have decided you need a time-out or a break from the demanding work of the season. You may need a "zest moment." You can add zest to your season—or someone else's season—by an act of kindness, a smile, a larger-than-normal tip.

My dad sacrificed more than once to add zest to our holidays. He believed in the promise of Jesus: "I am come that they might have life, and that they might have it more abundantly [zestfully]" (John 10:10, KJV). My father sampled the abundant life and now basks in eternal life. He discovered that Isaiah's "Prince of Peace" (9:6) brought that to those who followed Him.

# HOW TO PRAY
# THIS HOLIDAY SEASON

*Sit down, lie down, whatever position is
most comfortable. Be there. Be quiet. Be calm.
Be open. Pay no attention to your anxieties.
Don't resist them. Don't get in a fight with them.
Just ignore your fear of what might happen
this season without your loved one.
Call upon God as a loving God who loves
and cares for you. No matter how bad or
bleak things look this season, call upon this
God who loves you with an infinite love.
Breathe deeply, breathe calmly. Ask this loving God to help
you with whatever fear of anxiety you have* **this** *particular
day,* **this** *particular moment. . . .
Yes. No. Do I go to the Christmas reception at work?
Yes. No. Do I go to Phoenix and
spend Christmas with my children?
Just ask—no matter how small the issue.
Then wait. Wait quietly.
Breathe evenly, calmly.*
—Mitch Finley
*101 Ways to Nourish Your Soul,* 39

✳✳✳

*Thank you, Lord, for being interested in my grief.
Thank You, Lord, for enabling me to
sample joy during this season.*

✳✳✳

*Prayer of relinquishment for this holiday season:*
*I am numb with grief; keep your word, revive me!*
—The Psalter, Ps. 119:28

✳ ✳ ✳

*God, where are you in this?*
—Chittister, Joan. (2009 9 November). Lecture. Country Club Christian
Church, Kansas City, Missouri.

✳ ✳ ✳

*God, you are my Lord. Be true to your name,*
*show mercy and rescue me.*
—The Psalter, Ps. 109:21

✳ ✳ ✳

*Lord, this day, in this particular situation given*
*the circumstances as I understand them, I pray*
*for wisdom to know Your will, courage to do*
*Your will, strength to live with Your will. But I*
*need You to remind me that Your will is always,*
*always for my good.*
*In Jesus' name I pray. Amen.*

✳ ✳ ✳

*God, stay close.*
—*David Wolpe cited in Grossman (2008)*
[Wolpe, David]. Cited in Grossman, Cathy Lynn. (2008 22 September). Rabbi
Wolpe's "faith" takes on atheists and fanatics alike. USA Today, Electronic version.

# CONCLUSION

*I don't know how many more holiday seasons*
*I'll celebrate in this life. But I know that when*
*I wade the wide river into the real Kingdom,*
*every day will be Christmas!*
The Christmas carol "Joy to the World" suggests,
"Let **ev'ry** heart prepare Him room" (emphasis added).
*There's no asterisk to qualify the statement—as if saying,*
*"except for those who are grieving." There can come*
*those wonderful thin slices of life that*
*break through our despair, our grief.*
May this Christmas bring more wisdom to the way we look
at the world and more love to the way we live in it.
—Gerald & Betty Ford, Christmas 2006

Roberts, Cokie. (2006 27 December). Ford remembered for Nixon Pardon. NPR.
http://npr.org/templates/story. Php?storyId=6684841. Accessed January 17 2011.

*V*incent van Gogh's last words are what many grievers feel this season—especially this first season: *La tristesse durea*—"the sadness will never go away." It will not go away. But it will change. It will be muted. And at times it will go underground.

C. S. Lewis told the story of a woman who was thrown into a dark dungeon and eventually gave birth to a son. As the boy grew, she tried to explain to him about the outside world, the real world, where he would someday live. Many days she drew pictures. She assumed that he understood. He did not.

I like Ken Gire's interpretation of the story—we understand so little of eternity. We rely on some scriptures (sometimes lots of interpretation of those passages). What we need, Gire contends, is "to be boosted to a window [so that] we can see beyond the lines of our experience."

How many times, during our annual Christmas trip to see the trains at the downtown Sears store, I complained because of the crowd, "Daddy, I can't see!"

My dad would lift me to his shoulders. Ah—then I could see it.

At Christmas we find it hard to see because of the dark fog. What we need is Someone to lift us so that we *can* see.

After the death of his wife and children in a fire, song evangelist Luther B. Bridgers added a new verse to his popular song "He Keeps Me Singing":

> *Tho' sometimes he leads thro' waters deep,*
> *Trials fall across the way,*
> *Tho' sometimes the path seems rough and steep,*
> *See His footprints all the way.*

I would change the last line to read, "See! His footprints lead the way."

There is an advent of the heart, in the quiet corridors of your spirit, where no decorations clutter, where no fake Santa looks bored or weary, where no carolers stroll. There, in that quieted place, Advent is celebrated.

My wish for you is a moment, least expected, unplanned, perhaps at a point you need it most, when Someone will say, "Merry Christmas!"

And all the power of those two words will resound within your heart.

\* \* \*

*If we are still breathing, it is too early to tell the*
*ultimate impact of any event in our lives.*
—John Claypool
Claypool, John. (2005). *God the Ingenious Alchemist:*
*Transforming Tragedy into Blessing.* Harrisburg, PA: Morehouse, p. 40.

\* \* \*

*Memories of my loved one* . . .

# APPENDIX

## Recommended Resources on
## Dealing with Grief During the Holiday Season

Editors of Fairview Press. *Holiday Hope: Remembering Loved Ones During Special Times of the Year.* Minneapolis: Fairview Press, 1998. Available by phoning 219-424-7916.

Miller, James E. *How Will I Get Through the Holidays? 12 Ideas for Those Whose Loved One Has Died.* Fort Wayne, Ind.: Willowgreen Publishing, 1996.

Robinson, Jo, and Jean Coppock Staeheli. *Unplug the Christmas Machine: A Complete Guide to Putting Love and Joy Back into the Season.* Rev. ed. New York: William Morrow, 1991.

Zonnebelt-Smeenge, Susan J. & De Vries, Robert C. (2001). *The empty chair: Handling grief on holidays and special occasions.* Grand Rapids, MI: Baker Books.

# WORKS CITED

Alexander, Fran, ed. *Bloomsbury Keys: Quotations*. London: Bloomsbury, 1994.

Alexander, Victoria. *Words I Never Thought to Speak: Stories of Life in the Wake of Suicide*. New York: Lexington Books, 1991.

Anglican Church of Aotearoa, New Zealand, and Polynesia. *A New Zealand Prayer Book*. San Francisco: HarperCollins, 1997.

Ascher, Barbara Lazear. *Landscape Without Gravity*. Harrison, N.Y.: Delphium, 1992.

Beckett, Wendy. *A Child's Book of Prayer in Art*. London: Dorling Kindersley, 1995.

Benson, Peggy. *Listening for a God Who Whispers: A Woman's Discovery of Quiet Understanding*. Nashville: Generoux, 1991.

Bonhoeffer, Dietrich. *Meditating on the Word*. Ed. and trans. David McI. Gracie. Cambridge, Mass.: Cowley Publications, 1986.

*Book of Common Prayer: According to the Use of the Episcopal Church*. New York: Seabury, 1979.

Brener, Anne. *Mourning and Mitzvah: A Guided Journal for Walking the Mourner's Path Through Grief to Healing*. Woodstock, Vt.: Jewish Lights, 1993.

Camp, Wesley D. *Camp's Unfamiliar Quotations from 2000 B.C. to the Present*. Englewood Cliffs, N.J.: Prentice-Hall, 1990.

Capote, Truman. *The Thanksgiving Visitor* and *a Christmas Memory*. New York: Random House, 1967.

Cleckley, Mary. "What a Difference a Year Made." *Compassionate Friends* newsletter, Kansas City region, November 1995, 1.

Dargatz, Jan. *52 Simple Ways to Make Christmas Special*. Nashville: Oliver-Nelson, 1991.

Dickens, Charles. *A Christmas Carol*. New York: Random House, 1990.

Eyre, Richard. *Spiritual Serendipity: Cultivating and Celebrating the Art of the Unexpected*. New York: Simon and Schuster, 1997.

Finley, Mitch. *101 Ways to Nourish Your Soul*. New York: Crossroad, 1996.

Fitzgerald, Helen. *The Mourning Handbook*. New York: Simon and Schuster, 1994.

Foster, Richard. *Freedom of Simplicity*. San Francisco: Harper and Row, 1987.

Gire, Ken. *Windows of the Soul: Experiencing God in New Ways*. Grand Rapids: Zondervan, 1996.

Hudson, Lisa. "That's Just the Way Grief Is." *Forum,* November-December 1997, 3, 12-13.

Idle, Christopher, ed. *Christmas Carols and Their Stories.* Tring, Herts, England: Lion, 1988.

Kay, Alan A. *A Jewish Book of Comfort.* Northvale, N.J.: Jason Aronson, 1993.

Klug, Ron. *How to Keep a Spiritual Journal.* Nashville: Thomas Nelson, 1982.

Lawrence, Roy. *How to Pray When Life Hurts.* Downers Grove, Ill.: InterVarsity Press, 1993.

Manning, Doug. *Don't Take My Grief Away.* San Francisco: Harper and Row, 1979.

Miller, James E. *How Will I Get Through the Holidays? 12 Ideas for Those Whose Loved One Has Died.* Fort Wayne, Ind.: Willowgreen Publishing, 1996.

Muto, Susan A. *Pathways of Spiritual Living.* New York: Image/Doubleday, 1984.

Neeld, Elizabeth Harper. *Seven Choices: Taking the Steps to New Life After Losing Someone You Love.* New York: Delta-Dell, 1990.

Parachin, Victor. "What to Do When the Holidays Hurt." *Director,* December 1995, 50-51.

Peck, Emily Morison, ed. *Familiar Quotations: John Bartlett.* 15th ed. Boston: Little, Brown, 1980.

*Prayers of Those Who Mourn.* Chicago: Liturgical Training Publications, 1995.

Robinson, Jo, and Jean Coppock Staeheli. *Unplug the Christmas Machine: A Complete Guide to Putting Love and Joy Back into the Season.* Rev. ed. New York: William Morrow, 1991.

Rosten, Leo, ed. *Leo Rosten's Treasury of Jewish Quotations.* New York: Bantam, 1980.

Salamon, Julie. *The Christmas Tree.* New York: Random House, 1996.

Schlosser, Eric. "A Grief like No Other." *Atlantic Monthly,* September 1997, 50.

Schmitz, Barbara G. *The Life of Christ and the Death of a Loved One: Crafting the Funeral Homily.* Lima, Ohio: CSS Publishing, 1995.

"Sibling Grief." *Compassionate Friends* newsletter, Kansas City region, November 1994, 2-3.

Smith, Harold Ivan. *The Gifts of Christmas.* Kansas City: Beacon Hill Press of Kansas City, 1989.

Taylor, Barbara. *Mixed Blessings.* Atlanta: S. Hunter, 1996.

Tournier, Paul. *The Meaning of Persons.* New York: Harper and Row, 1975.

Vivas, Julie. *The Nativity.* San Diego: Harcourt Brace, 1986.

Weems, Ann. *Psalms of Lament*. Louisville, Ky.: Westminster John Knox Press, 1995.

Williams, Philip W. *When a Loved Ones Dies: Meditations for the Journey Through Grief*. Minneapolis: Augsburg Press, 1995.

Wirt, Sherwood Eliot, and Kersten Beckstrom, eds. *Topical Encyclopedia of Living Quotations*. Minneapolis: Bethany House, 1982.

Wojciechowski, Susan. *The Christmas Miracle of Jonathan Toomey*. Cambridge, Mass.: Candlewick Press, 1995.

Worden, J. William. *Grief Counseling and Grief Therapy: A Handbook for the Mental Health Practitioner*. 2nd ed. New York: Springer Publishing, 1991.

# ABOUT THE AUTHOR
# HAROLD IVAN SMITH

Harold Ivan Smith is a popular
speaker and grief educator.
He received his doctorate in
spiritual formation
from Asbury Theological Seminary.
Smith has published over 30
books and numerous articles.
He is a member of the Association
for Death Education and
Counseling and the National
Hospice Association's Council
of Professionals.

## Also by Harold Ivan Smith